CLOSE ENCOUNTERS
OF THE HOLIDAY KIND

Lester Gallagher

ISBN-13: 9798391013563

Cover design by: Art Painter
Library of Congress Control Number: 2018675309
Printed in the United States of America

"From there to here, and here to there, things are everywhere.

DR SEUSS

INTRODUCTION

"There's something incredibly exciting about booking a holiday. There are weeks of planning and research that go into ensuring that your getaway runs perfect. Those final days leading up to your holiday seem incredibly long and torturous. Suitcases have been packed and unpacked several times and the small check list has somehow turned into an excel spreadsheet. On the day you finally do set off, there's always that last minute obligatory check around the house. Heating off, check? Alarm on, check? Passports and money, check? Should we leave a light on? Not sure. Check, check, check! We all do it, because your first holiday disaster can happen before you've even set off. 'Stop, I've left the key in the front door. I think I've left the iron on. I forgot to put petrol in the car. Where's the taxi, they said he'd be here an hour ago?'It seems, that no matter how much pre planning we do, at some point the holiday gods will strike. Floods, fire, raging seas, it's no coincidence that the ancient Greeks attributed these events to supernatural beings that looked down upon us. Although we have a better understanding of the earth's atmosphere its "incredible that we dare to venture out of the front door. For many people, the perfect holiday consists of being baked, boiled and fried on a sun bed in the Mediterranean, it's just so appealing. In fact, peeling is something we British do amazingly well. We are more than willing to shed a few layers of skin towards gaining a leathered complexion in the quest of looking healthy. Travel, broadens the mind,' said the author and philosopher Aldous Huxley, who proved his words by travelling around Europe with his family during the early nineteen twenties. Although not a famous philosopher, I do have one thing in common with the man who wrote the widely acclaimed novel, 'Brave New World,' I too have dragged my family around Europe and beyond. Unlike the acclaimed author, we probably scrimped and saved a little bit harder for our annual family holiday. On numerous occasions, usually following a couple of drinks with friends, I've been told that I should put my own recollections into writing and share some of my not so wonderful holiday experiences. If like me, you can't help but laugh when people tell stories that caused embarrassment then I'm sure some of these accounts will help raise a smile. At the very least it will make you consider taking out a better insurance policy for your next holiday

◆ ◆ ◆

PREFACE

"The aim of this book was to bring together a collection of holiday stories that will take the reader on a journey of truly hilarious events. I'm talking about, the ones where you're not supposed to laugh. News readers call it 'Corpsing,' laughing at a story that's not supposed to be funny. The internet is full of clips were people trip, stumble and fall on holiday and although entertaining they lack intensity. Someone falls out of a hammock and that's it, you either find it hilarious or you don't. These small calamities are missing the human element and the thought process of the victim. The fear and loss of control described in the detail of a book allows us to live in the shoes of the author and feel their darkest emotions. I have neither the inclination nor courage to do 'stand up,' but i have done 'sit down.' I've told my stories to friend's over the years in pubs, hotels and even at work and I'm always met with the same reaction. 'You should write a book one day,' So, i did and i think it's got all the ingredients to take the reader on a journey of interesting places while ensuring many laugh out loud moments along the way. Just like a thriller at the cinema, the last two chapters of Close Encounters of the Holiday Kind, will leave you shocked or maybe in tears, followed by a chapter to knock your socks off."

TABLE OF CONTENTS

CHAPTER 1

Why Did That Chicken Cross The Road?

Born in the sixties as the son of a Bookmaker I was named Lester after the famous jockey Lester Piggott. My mother gave birth to me at our home in Ellesmere Port and we later moved to Knotty Ash in Liverpool. My childhood was a blur, and I certainly didn't have the aspirations to follow in my namesakes' legendary footsteps. The closest I came to riding a Derby winner was at a donkey derby in Llandudno, North Wales. I also rode a camel which turned out to be a terrifying trip into the unknown, which I will cover during a later chapter. In my youth, the nearest thing i could relate to a holiday, was a stay at my aunties house in Cumbria. She lived not far from the beach, and it was idyllic in comparison to our corner house in Liverpool which we shared with a large family of mice. By the age of nine my father had landed a job in Llandudno, which as mentioned previously is a small holiday resort on the North Wales coast. Still a 'Bookie,' he worked every Saturday, so we saw very little of him except on a Sunday, where it was odds on, he'd be nursing a hangover. When we asked him if we could go on holiday like the other kids, he'd say, 'you live in a holiday town, you're already on bloody holiday.' I was always envious when I heard about the other kids in my school going abroad to places like Torremolinos or Benidorm. Even the kids who told me they were going to Talacre made me imagine some far off exotic place. Little did I know that it was only twenty five miles down the coast. My wife, Diane, had also grown-up watching people like Judith Chalmers showing us the kind of places that were far beyond our budget, especially for a family with three children. By the mid eighties, long time favourites such as Butlins and Pontins were beginning to look old and tired, and flights abroad were starting to become far more affordable. Hotels offering sun, sea and sangria were becoming no more expensive than staying in the UK. After searching through brochure after brochure the only thing they all had in common was, you never quite knew what you were getting. These were the days before the internet, therefore word of mouth and the travel rep was the only reliable source of information you could depend on. Most of the holiday brochures gave you two pictures, one of the pool and one of the room. A little bit of glorified information accompanied a facilities list and that was it. Working overtime to pay off your holiday was the norm, and Saturday mornings paid at time and a half soon became your regular hours. The brochures were always full of glossy photographs showing blue sky destinations and immaculate hotels. The wording was designed to pull at your conscience and in most cases it worked. *'Taking your children on holiday is the ultimate family adventure and should allow you to devote all your energy to those that matter the most.'* What they didn't tell you, is that being on holiday in unfamiliar surroundings completely changes the dynamics and keeping your family safe is suddenly harder than when you're at home. For starters there's a great big swimming pool that my kids found irresistible even without their armbands on. There's slippy floors, food poisoning, diarrhoea and sun burn, everything you need to guarantee a trip to the local pharmacy? Our family holidays often took me to the brink of despair and if there's one golden rule all parents should remember, is that teenagers will be teenagers. However, before I blame my children for every misadventure that ever happened on holiday let me state for the record, it didn't change when it became only me and the wife. As much as I thought that going on holiday as a couple would be far easier, I couldn't have been more wrong.

At sixty years of age, i still get that giddy feeling the night before a holiday. The excitement, the adventure and the impending freedom, I can't wait to set off for the airport. As you work your way through the chapters of this book, you may begin to ask yourself why?

Have you ever wondered how you managed to survive those certain moments in your life that had intensive care written all over them? Most of us have fallen off a bike at some time but didn't break any bones. What about the time you stepped into the road and came face to face with the Grim Reaper? Mr Reaper was innocently driving his Nissan Skyline and you were on your phone texting omg lol, and so was he. It could have been D.O.A, in A & E, Wtf! There are many unusual tales of how certain people died in strange or bizarre fashions. It seems that life is full of perilous and dangerous moments that we constantly manage to swerve by luck or by design. The simple coconut is said to be responsible for around one hundred and fifty deaths a year. My dad always said being alive is dangerous. The fact is I've run into more hazard's on holiday than I ever did at home apart from the time when i plumbed the washing machine into the gas. My love of traveling has given me the opportunity to visit some amazing destinations with famous historical sites attached to them. I do love a bit of history and will make time for a visit to any old, ruined site or museum. Sounds a bit boring but stick with me i just may change your opinion.

Is there a greater city on earth that holds more impressive monuments than those in Rome?

This beautiful city is crammed full of historical buildings which nestle easily and elegantly between the modern architecture of today. Staying in a small hotel on the outskirts of the city we were lucky to be located near to a train station that was within a short walking distance. Travelling with our friends we'd arrived early in the morning and wasted little time in setting off for the heart of the city.

I'm not the least bit religious but the Vatican was to be our first port of call when we arrived in the heart of this bustling capital. We paid €6.66 to get into the famous holy landmark, 'ker-ching.' At €6.66 you think they would have played safe and changed it to

€6.67. I gazed in awe at the ceiling of the Sistine chapel, while being encouraged to move along with the ever surging crowd. As I stared at the 'Creation of Adam,' painted by the great Michael Angelo, I remember asking myself is this what God would really look like? The famous painting depicts the almighty stretching out a finger to touch Adam and God is clearly a man. That's not to say God couldn't be or a woman, a woman can have a beard, I've watched 'The Greatest Showman.' However, the one thing you can't help but notice within the walls of the Vatican is its display of masculinity. The marble statues of historical figures portraying wisdom or athleticism all possessing a six pack and thankfully a small penis.   Let's face it you never know if your wife is being judgemental. The huge paintings and tapestries that cover the walls depict various biblical events. Every doorway opens up into another room that isn't too dissimilar to the previous room, an Alzheimer's sufferers nightmare. I could only compare it to the palace of Versailles, which was built on the over taxation and starvation of the poorest people of France. I found the Vatican to be remarkably lavish for a holy establishment, and the colour of gold seemed to be more prevalent than any other. In contrast, a few days later I visited a small church in Venice and quietly observed its patrons worshipping in a far less ornate building. It asked for nothing, except for respect. A private sermon was about to begin, and we were asked to leave, with the door being gently closed behind us. Religion and money certainly work in mysterious ways. On my travels I've learnt that the thing that sets us apart as human beings, is sometimes nothing more than our languages and beliefs.   Inside every border of every country, you will find extreme poverty and astonishing wealth, along with unusual ceremonies and customs. One thing is for certain, , everybody dances, and everybody sings. No matter where you go, people have one thing in common and that is the ability to smile and point you in the right direction. Sadly, that is not always the case, and the world can be a tricky place to navigate, never more so than when you're on holiday.

For instance, the phrase, 'Force Majeure,' are two words that we smartly adopted into the English language. For starters it's French and who doesn't admire the smooth eloquence of the French language? 'Je ne sais quoi,' I don't know what that means but it sounds bloody marvellous. The French also gave us 'Vol au vent' along with some other tasty morsels from their Latin combinations. Force Majeure is for all intended purposes the stealth phrase of the lucrative insurance companies. If like me, you suddenly feel the urge to read the terms and conditions of your holiday insurance policy before You travel, then let me explain what prompted you. On the verge of setting off for the airport you suddenly want to know what will happen if you miss your flight? This moment of self-induced panic was brought to you by Malcolm, the IT guy at work, who recently told you he'd missed his flight to Comic Con. This was due to a lorry crash on the M6 which created a two-hour tail back to Manchester Airport. On other trips he was delayed because of fog and the mechanical failure due to ice? Suddenly everybody took the opportunity to join Malcolm in regaling stories of their own misfortunes when traveling to the airport. There was also the curious situation of when a co-pilot had a 'nervous breakdown in the cockpit of an Air Canada flight to Heathrow. It was reported that on a January morning in 2008, a co-pilot had to be dragged from the cockpit and handcuffed to a chair whilst he was shouting 'I need to talk to God.' There are a million reasons why your flight to warmer climates might not get off the ground and let me assure you it's not always an act of god. Look closely and you will find the terrifying scenarios which are clearly written in the small print of your insurance policy using the font size known as minuscule. Hidden in plain sight is a part that will alert you to the fact that *no payments shall be made due to terrorism or explosions, hi jacks or lightning strikes that might disable the aircraft.'* It's the part that slaps you in the face for having the audacity to read the bit that they thought you would never read. If you happen to be onboard a plane where you suddenly find yourself at the mercy of a terrorist attack or a hi jacking, you won't be thinking, let's have a quick look at that policy again. Getting on a plane is something many people fear regardless of the nightmare scenarios mentioned. For some and that also includes the writer, there is a morbid fear of flying. Yes, we've all heard the statements that are supposed to put you at ease with the concept of hurtling through the air at thirty-five thousand feet in a smartie tube. The ones that begin with, 'you've got more chance of getting hit by a bus or winning the lottery. How I hate this whimsical remark, because plenty of people do get hit by a bus and someone in the world wins the lottery every week. So, what is it that makes people like me feel that flying is the equivalent of throwing a chicken off the top of Empire State Building? The answer is rather simple. A chicken has wings, feathers and a beak, but it lacks one major feature, it can't fly. No matter how high you take it, it's going to plummet beak first into the pavement below. A Peregrine falcon has the same attributes and flies at around two hundred miles per hour. Chickens are definitely at the bottom of the pecking order when it comes to getting off the ground but they sure are tasty. This leaves them with the prospect of being stuffed and shoved into a hot oven. Which, coincidentally is like economy class on most planes. Let me take you through the mind of the frequent flyer who hates getting inside any vehicle that doesn't keep its wheels on the ground. The common denominator when it comes to overcoming the fear of flying is the desire to escape this shitty rain-soaked country and to get fried on a sun lounger. Most nervous flyers are superstitious and have developed little traits that are designed to ward off evil spirits, except those served in flight. Saint Christopher pendants adorn the neck of many an anxious passenger who believes that this will guarantee them safe passage to their final destination. This patron saint of travellers, is usually depicted as holding a small child and guiding them to safety. Saint Christopher, according to the history books, was beheaded when he visited Lycia in 251 AD. That's the equivalent of being a rabbit and carrying a lucky rabbit's foot. Without doubt some nervous passengers will suddenly turn to God while sat in the window seat of row thirteen. The Lord's Prayer is a take-off favourite, hopefully not to be repeated mid journey. It is estimated that there are roughly twenty thousand flights in the skies at any one time so the chances of God tuning into those prayers are pretty slim. When boarding the aircraft, the nervous flyer will scrutinise the seats which can help alleviate some fears, especially if they look new. The conflicting argument to a superstitious flyer would be, that an older plane must surely be more reliable. If it's an older plane, could it be about to fall apart due to excessive vibration and millions of air miles? More questions arrive from the back of your mind, like, when was it last maintained, is that really a crack in the window? The fear of flying is an excruciating dilemma and is usually it at its peak just before take-off. Watching the hustle and bustle of fellow passengers pushing down the isles carrying their hand luggage makes the thought of leaving an impossibility. The desperation to get their extra hand luggage into a compartment above their seat, is their only priority. Anyone blocking the isle could cause mayhem stretching back beyond the aircraft door. The objective here is to get us sat down as quickly as they can and buckled up. The crew will then give us a choreographed demonstration of what to do in an emergency which you can't decide whether you should look or pretend to be busy? When they finish their serious but slower version of YMCA, the fearful flyer now feels as deflated as the yellow life jacket around the cabin crew's neck. Ironically the specially trained cabin Crewe are more fearful of the passengers than they are of turbulence or crashing. The thought of plummeting into a steep ninety-degree angle towards death is the last thing on their minds. The one person the terrified flyer doesn't want to see, is the pilot. A forty-year-old pilot is the equivalent of Flash Gordon to a sixty-year-old passenger. A thirty-year-old pilot is a boy racer and a woman flying a plane is going to make it the longest journey on earth. Sexist pig I hear you say, but don't be too quick to judge. I'm not sexist at all, women are in many respects braver, stronger and more resilient than men. Women have conquered space, made it to prime minister in many countries and are top surgeons and great scientists, my mum was a woman too. I want the pilot to be my age, at whatever age I'm at, but that stops at sixty five. I want him to have the handlebar moustache and that great calming voice that's smoothly hypnotic. He's the guy who, if needs be, will land the plane safely on water, while both engines are on fire. He could have been blinded by the scalding tea that fell off his dashboard and still land on the A55 to north Wales. I don't want to hear the words turbulence or severe weather during mid-flight and not from a pilot with a Brummie or a Scouse accent either. I have a Scouse accent, my mother and my father and both sets of my grandparents were scousers along with some of my grandchildren too. My wife was born in Liverpool, so don't even think of throwing the stereotypical accusations at me. I once took a flight from Coventry to Jersey with a Scouse pilot at the helm and I struggled to take his announcements seriously. I remember the take-off dialogue sounding something like, *'alright, use are in for a quick flight today. D' tail wind is blowing like billio, so I reckon it woan even take us an hour.' We're just waiting for clearance and then we can go ed and get this big bird off da' ground.'* This person may have been the greatest pilot in the UK, but the accent just didn't work for me. I know its wrong, but i associate certain accents with stereotypes and that's due to television and celebrities. I find the Brummie accent makes me laugh and I can never take it seriously. People from Birmingham have a great sense of humour, but yow don't see them reading the news on the BBC. The same can be said for many other English dialects, including people from Wales and Scotland.

So, rule one, the pilot must sound like Lawrence Olivier or Kenneth Branagh playing Henry the V rallying his troops. When booking my seat, I prefer to be sitting in an aisle seat just in case I have to rugby tackle a would be 'hi jacker.' No, I'm not saying I'm Bruce Willis, aka - John MacLaine, but I've decided I'm going to scream uncontrollably as I hurl myself at their feet and beg for mercy, therefore creating a distraction with the hope that there happens to be a few rugby players on board. Alternatively, I will go to the toilet at the first sign of trouble and lock myself in before anyone else does. The biggest fear I do have is the command to 'brace, brace, brace.' This is were we struggle to remember the flight crew's specific instructions at the beginning of the flight. 'Should we find it necessary to land on water there is a life jacket under your seat.' Really......? Who the fuck are they kidding? If you dropped a large fluorescent light bulb under your seat, you wouldn't find it again or have enough room to pick it up. I'm frightened to take my shoes off on a flight as they are impossible to put back on. Let's face it, three people with the same build as the front row of a British Lions scrum are not going to have enough room to bend over and find their life jackets under their seats. They may be there, I've never seen them, but logistics tell us, it just won't work. On some larger planes there are four people in the middle rows which makes even going the toilet a bloody chore. While the plane is in an uncontrollable flat spin somewhere over the mid-Atlantic, most normal people will be completely disoriented and screaming hysterically. Can you really expect them to suddenly start using good manners while getting their life jackets? 'After you, no after you.' 'No after you I insist.' 'Have you managed to find yours?' 'Yes, I have thank you.' 'That's good, now don't forget, you're not to pull the, (pssshhh) oh you already have, never mind were all going to fucking die anyway.' We are asked to observe the glossy diagram in the back of the seat in front of us, demonstrating the crash position which involves sticking your head between your knees and kissing your arse goodbye. The only people I've ever seen adopt this position have been on the Royal Variety Show. They call themselves contortionists and often fold their body into a small box the size of a microwave on stage for public entertainment. I have come to realise over the years that the pre take off safety routine is essentially a calming technique. It's to stop mass hysteria and the uncomfortable realisation that you and the Empire State chicken are of a similar design, both stuffed, and in the event of an emergency, it won't be eggs your laying. In my early thirties i attended an offshore survival course, which included an upside down underwater helicopter escape. Trust me, trying to climb out of a small window with a helideck suit on is the stuff of nightmares. Knowing when to take that last breath and waiting to be rolled upside down is the slowest moment of time you can ever experience. You pray that the seat belt clasp will undo, and the window handle will allow it to be opened. Then you must squeeze out through this small opening like you are being born all over again in a birthing pool. When you reach the surface, the instructors give you a de brief and mention that the chances of surviving a similar crash in the North Sea are virtuously impossible.

I've been on so many flights over the years that I now have an acute ability to spot or sense a potential issue. Not just inside the aircraft but on the outside too. Gazing out of the window one cold January morning on the runway of Manchester airport, I could see a thin layer of ice on the wings of our Delta Airways flight to New York. Five minutes later the captain was leaning on my chair looking out of my window saying, 'I think I'll get some spray on them,' I think I nodded as if I'd brought it to his attention. It's not just aircraft that have given me some worrying moments, it's shared out equally amongst other forms of transport too. I've also been on the receiving end of quite a few near misses, including falling out of a fairground ride whilst upside down and nearly drowning on more than one occasion.

I realised many years ago that there was a good reason why you need insurance when travelling, especially when it's anything that can be defined as a family holiday. Our first family holiday was to the 'Siesta apartments,' in northern Spain. In the early eighties Parafrugel was a quaint fishing village situated on the northern coast of Costa Brava. My wife had booked the holiday and we spent many weeks meticulously planning every step of our forthcoming journey. Parafrugel was actually pronounced parra-fru-shell and not parra-frugle, which is what we had been calling it since paying our deposit. This was to be our first steps into the world of global travel, the Gallaghers were officially part of the jet set. Setting off early we arrived excitedly at Manchester airport and joined the check in queue with our two boys Paul and Adam who were aged three and four. Before leaving home that morning, I had discovered a secret compartment underneath one of our travel bags. This bag had already been packed with all of our essentials. Those essentials included a couple of loose toilet rolls as we must have thought they may not have any toilet paper in Spain.

As we approached the check in my wife asked me to hand her the passports. I opened the bag and went to the side zip where my wife had carefully placed them days earlier, only to find that they had somehow disappeared. I began to frantically search through the rest of the baggage, quickly becoming aware that all eyes were now upon us. My wife stared at me with an expression that had volcano written all over it. My mother-in-law who'd kindly joined us for this trip, smiled knowingly with her fork tongue rapidly slipping back and forth. The queue had quickly caught on to my dilemma and was more interested in my fate than advancing towards the check in desk. My wife was now speaking to me through gritted teeth like an angry ventriloquist and it was at this point a toilet roll tumbled out of the bag and set off like a ten-pin bowling ball towards the check in desks. It rolled effortlessly past the entire length of the queue as if being chased by a cute Labrador puppy. My brain went into overdrive trying to calculate how long it would take me to get home in a taxi. What if I couldn't find the passports? What if I didn't get back in time? It was like number crunching in an episode of Countdown, what would Carol Vorderman do? An hour to get home, an hour to get back, plus some extra time to ransack the house. It's around this point my wife was allowing people in the queue to step in front of us. The blood was draining from my face, but it continued to radiate with the same colour it should have been on day two of my holiday. I do have an amazing ability to burn my face no matter how much care I take in the sun. Like a condemned man remembering where he was on the night of the murder, I suddenly remembered the secret compartment. I unzipped it and pulled out the passports and held them up to the crowd as if to expect a cheer or some celebration. I'd just been handed a pardon on death row for god's sake, but the spectators seemed disappointed. My wife smiled at me and said, 'silly you, fancy putting them there,' or something along those lines.

I was never allowed to have the passports again, well not for many years. Passports can cause so many issues I often wonder why we haven't found a better solution. We now go through the commotion of stripping off like your about to get a rapid prostrate examination. Young or old, disabled or in a wheelchair, it's belts off, shoes off, no watches, I pad's in the tray, no jewellery, and nothing over fifty mills. Airport security staff are shouting at you to place everything in a plastic tray and move along, it's slightly reminiscent of Schindler's list. Not the nicest analogy, but tell me where else this happens? While trying to keep those comfortable extra-large pants from falling down with one hand, passport control asks you to raise your arms before walking through the detector. It's organised chaos and much worse if they randomly slide your tray to one side. After a quick frisk by the attendant, we meet up with our confiscated hand luggage. A cheery soul who lost his last job as a traffic warden calls you over to examine the case with him. 'Are these your items sir?' You try to smile innocently as you confirm that you are indeed the owner of the opened suitcase with three packets of Imodium on display. It's difficult to describe but we all get that subconscious thought that says, I'm guilty of something but I don't know what it is yet. The scene from the film Midnight Express is lurking somewhere in the corner of your mind. What have they found? Has someone planted a few grams of cocaine into my box of pringles? 'Did you pack this bag yourself sir?' This is the bit where if you're a bloke you have no choice but to lie. 'Yes, I did, is there a problem?' As a grown man I don't feel comfortable telling the security person that my wife packed my bag along with some clean underpants and a pair of flamingo patterned trunks that looked great on the plus sized model in the Jacamo advert. I do accept that women are somehow skilled in the art of organisation and let's face it the last thing on my mind was having enough deodorant to last for ten days. My holiday checklist consists of, two pairs of trunks, two pairs of shorts and the underpants I'm wearing. When Noah loaded the ark, I'm sure his wife wasn't checking if he had enough socks for the journey.

We have all come to accept the heightened security associated with an airport and it has become a necessary requirement in the world of travel. This holiday was during the times of perhaps less scrutiny or should i say less security. I remember how we dashed through the airport with the intention of being at the front of the queue to get on the plane. We arrived at the boarding gate with two sleepy children eager to get onto our evening flight.   Our first flight together would last no longer than two and a half hours, but we were beyond excited. The flight attendant greeted us onto the small plane and then instantly put her hand up to halt the other passengers behind us. The pilot had suddenly appeared from the cockpit and had spoken to her in a calm but authoritative manner. She made an apology and asked the queue of passengers to make their way back to the waiting area as a technical issue had been encountered. I have come to understand over many years that a 'technical issue,' is the pilot's code word for, 'this plane needs to be fixed because not flying it otherwise.'

We, on the other hand were already seated, buckled up and ready for take-off. She spoke once more to the pilot and then turned to us with one of those highly trained reassuring smiles. 'You may as well stay where you are. We are just changing a flat tyre it won't take too long.' It's a strange feeling knowing that no one else was allowed to board the plane and yet here we were sitting alone with the plane completely to ourselves apart from the Crew. What happened next was also slightly unnerving. I felt the plane getting jacked up right beneath us and could hear the mechanics doing a wheel change. It sounded identical to when you get a tyre changed at your local garage and so began my fear of flying. I wanted the boys to be excited watching the plane take off into the night sky, but the worry that the wheel may not have been bolted back on correctly began to dance in and out of my thoughts. To add to this irrational fear came a new twist, one that had probably more weight and importance. Two passengers had not boarded the plane although they had been confirmed as checked in. The pilot made an announcement and explained to all the passengers with a degree of irritation in his voice, that we will be almost certainly delayed if they fail to appear. He mentioned that all the luggage would need to be removed from the plane to find the missing passengers belongings before the plane would be allowed to take off. This was probably my first encounter with the effects of terrorism, apart from dodging the local gangs in my youth during the weekly outbreak of fighting at my local pub. Eventually, two slightly overweight and out of breath fifty-year-olds finally arrived at the plane door gasping for breath and mouthing red-faced apologies. Think, Christopher Biggins and Melissa McCarthy and you'll get the picture. The pilot who was not impressed at being made to wait and having to repeatedly explain the situation over the PA, decided to personally greet these two stragglers. They were sat directly opposite to us near the door, so I was close enough to witness and enjoy the full-blown wrath of the pilot. Scolded like children and given a lesson in aviation costs he didn't hold back. He explained how much a new take off slot costs and the inconvenience they'd caused to all the other passengers. Red faced they stared at the pilot as he finished by saying, 'sit down, and don't move until we tell you to.'

By the time we did start finally moving, my two boys had fallen fast asleep. I desperately wanted them to be awake and in truth I wanted them to be as excited as I was. Sadly, it was too late, they were at that stage were no number of gentle nudges would stir them from their slumber. So, I watched alone, still excited, but from the aisle seat it would be hard to see and appreciate that first take off experience. My darling wife always volunteered to sit next to the stranger on the plane so found herself seated one row behind us. I personally find it slightly uncomfortable sitting arm to arm next to another person that I've never met before. You never quite know who has the ownership of the arm rest that divides you. I once sat on the very back row of a plane between my wife and another woman and managed to spill not one but two glasses of red wine over a complete stranger. Worse still, they were her drinks not mine. Anyone old enough to remember the great Leonard Rossiter and Joan Collins in the Cizano Bianco advert will know exactly how I felt. She was very forgiving and made light of my clumsiness although her clothes were probably ruined by an extortionately charged red Merlot.

The plane slowly began to manoeuvre towards the position of take-off. I was absolutely shattered by this point and the last few days of working overtime, and the overall holiday preparation had finally caught up with me. The ability to fall into a state of hypnagogic sleep has been with me all my life. I often fight hard against going to sleep and therefore my head must be falling off my shoulders before I surrender. 'Sleep those little slices of death, how I loathe them' a very apt quote in my case, which is attributed to Edgar Alan Poe

Somewhere between drowsy and asleep, I begin to mix reality up with subconscious thoughts. The two states begin to blend like a drop of ink in a bottle of water. An example of this would be, a real knock at the door will invoke a person knocking on a door in my dream. In other words, I'll fit the dream to whatever I can hear around me. I often know that I'm dreaming, and it can be quite alarming as I try to wake myself up. I occasionally shout out to my wife to wake me up and amazingly she sometimes hears me. This must be how Wes Craven got the idea for the movie 'A Nightmare on Elm Street.

I hadn't realised that our flight to Costa Brava was now gaining momentum, since I was now drifting in and out of this dreamlike state. The engines roared and whistled at a high pitch before rushing purposefully towards the end of the runway. I opened my eyes from what had probably been nothing more than two-minutes' worth of disoriented sleep. Straining my neck from my isle seat I could just see small lights illuminated below the plane. The boys looked strangely comfortable and yet given their posture they shouldn't have been. Paul and Adam were slumped over their arm rests disappointingly sound asleep. I'm intensely jealous of anyone who can sleep on a plane, let alone my own two children. I don't resent anyone getting some much-needed rest, I just hate the fact that I can't do the same. To be able to have someone wake you up and say, 'we're here,' must be glorious. Those sci fi films were they're heading for Mars and the crew have all been put into a deep sleep chamber for the whole journey, would be perfect for long haul flights. Curiously, most of those sci fi journeys into space are often ruined by a close encounter of the gruesome kind. The slogan for the 1979 film 'Alien,' was, *no one will hear you scream,'* which may be true in outer space, but on a plane, if you scream, everyone will hear it. I'll explain this in more detail later and prove that my fear of flying is totally justified. Fortunately, there was to be no screaming on this flight, however on a future flight to Venice there was to be plenty. Apart from the initial boarding hic ups this flight was going to be uneventful, and we were now making our way to Parafrugel. I continued to strain my neck towards the outside world which was devoid of any natural light or recognisable landscape. Looking for all the world like an inquisitive tortoise I could hear the rumble of fresh new tyres rolling along Manchester's runway two. Then to my delight I could see the warm yellow lights of the houses below or perhaps they were the motorway lamps of the M56 glowing in a translucent straight line. The aircraft engines suddenly gave a mighty roar that answered the command for more power and within seconds the nose of the aircraft pointing towards the evening sky. The take-off angle of an aeroplane is somewhere around ten degrees when it finally musters up the immense strength needed to leave the ground. It's a moment that creates a state of mixed emotions for so many people. Joy, excitement, and fear, all the ingredients normally associated with a roller coaster ride. I had wanted to fall asleep and join my two boys doing what tortoises do best, but I couldn't, I never could. I came to realise that the small lights that I'd took for distant earthly objects were in fact the runway lights. I was not in control of the situation and some people were cheering, but I didn't understand why. A short time later i over heard a voice from the seat in front of me say, 'if we're going to die it's normally on take-off that's the most dangerous part.' I stared between the seats at the owner of this voice of doom and wondered why he would loudly announce such a demoralising fact and hoped a flight attendant would stick some duct tape over his big mouth. I also wondered why he needed to announce this shitty fact just as we were heading into the night sky. The facts of doom were coming from a spotty student, whose face I can still see clearly today. I don't know why but his cruel affliction of acne seemed to suit his persona. I guessed that he was aged somewhere between eighteen and twenty-one. If you'd have joined up the spots on his forehead it would have have spelt the word knob head right across his annoying toothy face. His thick rimmed glasses and his black curly hair gave him a resemblance to the character 'where's Wally.' But this Wally hadn't finished impressing his besotted student girlfriend. She gazed lovingly into his eyes as he started to create his own version of University Challenge. 'Starter for ten, what is the second most dangerous part of a flight?' I had stupidly caught his eye, so he was now aware of a growing audience. 'I don't know Jeremy, turbulence or engine fire,' his girlfriend laughed as if to make light of her terrifying reply. She had a laugh that resembled a machine gun with a multitude of pig like snorts in-between. With simple intuition the merchant of doom had detected a notion of fear in my sullied expression. Maybe it was the grip I had on my chair that gave me away initially, or perhaps the jaw dropping Jacob Marley impression I was doing? I don't know exactly what inspired him, but he took the opportunity to spout even more of his reasons to be fearful. 'It's the landing,' he said with a tone that sounded like an undertaker consoling a bereaved relative. He had purposely changed his demeanour to emphasise this point and I'm sure he was hoping to get at least some reaction from me. He continued with his Bamber Gascoigne impression, 'they've got to get the wheels down and sometimes one of the wheels won't lock into place. If you must land on one wheel it will tip you to one side and possibly cause an engine fire which will ignite the fuel. You won't get off the plane in time and you will probably burn to death or die of smoke inhalation.' His girlfriend reacted with a fretful sigh and looked at me and said, 'how awful.' I had joined their conversation without saying a word. I wasn't about to fan the flames of his morbid fascination with another question. But I had become engrossed by his sermon, I was easy prey. I wanted him to say something along the lines of 'don't worry we're on the Boeing 767, which has never had a single crash in twenty years. It has two of the finest Rolls Royce engines and my father personally knows the pilot and he's the trainer for all other pilots.' But this clever bastard never knew when to shut up.

I gripped the arms of my seat like John coffee in 'The Green Mile,' terrified for the remainder of the entire journey. I've heard some people say, 'I don't think the electric chair would be a painful way to die.' My answer to this would be, 'really, have you tried it?' All I needed for a complete breakdown was for turbulence to make an appearance. Up until this point I'd only seen it in films, mostly disaster movies and it always looked like the plane was going break into jagged pieces. How can anyone honestly say they are not disturbed by turbulence? I don't like driving down a bumpy road never mind being thrown around at thirty thousand feet. I'm pleased to say my worries were not justified and two hours later we landed on a rain-soaked runway in Costa Brava. Girona airport to be exact, were *the rain in Spain was all over my plane.* This was definitely not in the brochure.

So far, everything I'd seen and read about Spain was testimony to its permanent blue skies and its dry hot weather. The glossy Thomas Cook literature had virtually sold us a return trip to paradise and I wasn't packing a raincoat. Toilet rolls, yes, but anything that hinted at dress wear for campers or labelled as waterproof, didn't make the suitcase. It was near to midnight when we docked at the inbound gantry, so perhaps it just rained in the night i thought? The passage through the airport was difficult but I was glad to have my feet firmly on the ground. I had no choice but to carry my two sleeping toddlers over each shoulder and watch my wife drag two over weight suitcases now brandishing tickets saying 'heavy.' Back in the early eighties, I don't think there were any strict rules regarding excess baggage. You virtually tore both hamstrings lifting your suitcase onto the scales at the check in desk. You smiled at the check in person and held up your cute kids to their eye level and hoped for a smile. We didn't pay for pre booking seats, nor did they fine you for being over by a few extra kilos. I don't recall any planes not being able to take off due to the weight of the suitcases. Every passenger was guilty of packing the equivalent of a small car engine into their suitcases and nobody asked questions. You could take liquids in your hand luggage and duty free was duty free. Even worse was the fact that there was smoking allowed on planes up until the late eighties.

British Airways introduced non-smoking flights in 1990 and thereafter most other companies followed suit. Pilots were allowed to continue smoking in the cockpit for a brief time, as it was a considered opinion that the sudden withdrawal symptoms and deprivation of nicotine may affect their performance. I remember people smoking on planes and I also remember glancing backwards at the cloud of constant smog that hung over the back twenty rows of seats. The flight attendant, or trolly dolly's as they were called, would appear from the acrid grey plume like a west end theatre singer about to do a rendition of the Phantom of the Opera. Cigarettes were sold in vast quantities along with alcohol and other genuine offers. Travellers could buy copious quantities of booze and thousands of cigarettes at the airport and then buy more alcohol and cigarettes at duty free prices on the plane. Most people then topped up their supplies with even more cut-price cigarettes and spirits at their destination. Finding room in the suitcase for the sangria and two thousand cigarettes on the way home was a creative challenge. Most entrepreneurs succeeded, some even gave up other belongings such as towels and clothing to make the necessary room. During our holiday in Parafrugel we met a family who were dead ringers for the Trotter family from Only Fools and Horses. We met them while we were waiting to be picked up by the coach for the return journey to the airport. This was long before the average holiday maker would consider hiring a car or take a taxi. I sat in a lobby that was full of red-faced adults and restless children who couldn't understand why they couldn't go into the swimming pool one more time. Sitting directly opposite, were three men who closely resembled Rodney, Grandad and Del Boy from the series of only fools and horses. Grandad was sat in a wheelchair with the lower half of his leg cased in plaster. The youngest man of the three didn't speak, he just looked out of the atrium window with a slightly withdrawn demeanour. The other man whom I guessed was the older brother had a solid familiar cockney accent. His appearance reminded me of someone who in his younger days may have been into heavy metal. He had long thinning greasy hair and wore a leather waist coat. His only similarity to Del Boy apart from the accent was that he wore a long chunky gold necklace. After a couple of nods and smiles in my direction, the older brother struck up conversation. 'You got yourself plenty of faaags?' He asked this with a degree of expectancy in a strong cockney accent. I told him I'd got about five hundred and he instantly gave a shocked reaction. 'Fack orf, you're avin me on ain't cha?' He gave a broad smile revealing a set of heavily stained and yellowing teeth. 'My wife doesn't smoke and I only smoke about ten a day,' I felt as if I needed to apologise for my good behaviour. He went on to explain how his father had broken his foot due to being 'fackin Scotch Mist and putting one of his 'plates of meat' down an open grid. Adding insult to injury it had also cost him a small fortune to get it sorted and plastered.

He then lightened the mood after frowning at his father and calling him a dopey old git. 'We've shoved abat' two hundred faaags' inside that plaster ain't we dad?' He was delighted at his own ingenuity and thought this was highly amusing. His father nodded, smiled and pointed down to the side of his cast. His father actually resembled Leonard Pierce, the actor who played Del Boys grandfather. I could see the top part of a packet of cigarettes just level with the opening area of the rim of plaster. I couldn't fathom how they'd managed to fit two hundred cigarettes around what looked to be a snug almost tight-fitting support. It never dawned on me that they were all wearing sombrero's, I almost half expected it. They were every inch the British traveller I'd seen on the sit coms of the seventies. This being the eighties they stood out as a little bit dated. Even more astonishing, and cringe worthy was the fact they were lugging a Spanish donkey around with them. Fluffy dice was definitely in the car back home. They came across as perfect extras for a carry-on abroad film and they were probably good fun to be around. It would not have surprised me if these guys had unknowingly met up with John Sullivan the writer and creator of 'Only Fools and Horses, providing him with the inspiration. Then came the crem de la crem, although again it should not have come as any surprise. The eldest son with almost surgical precision lifted his father's sombrero carefully in a vertical motion. Balanced intricately on his father's head was a column of cigarettes. Grandad was as still as a corpse; he never moved his head one millimetre. His son gave another toothy grin and managed to lift his own sombrero at the same time but not as high. At this point it looked like a magicians trick, the famous cup and balls. The youngest man who was taking little interest in his older brothers' confessions, turned towards me when he heard his name called and pointed at his own sombrero. Sometime later I wondered how they'd got on with their smuggling attempts. If caught, I thought customs would either stick a heavy fine on them or possibly die laughing. They also told me about the thousands of cigarettes they had in their suitcases and how it would pay for their next holiday. I couldn't help but hope they'd got away with it.

Parafrugel had given us our first taste of a family holiday abroad. The rain decided to stay on the plane, and we were welcomed by hot blistering sunshine from day one. The Siesta complex was a mixture of wooden cabins and brick type chalets, the kind you would have seen in Butlins during the nineteen sixties. We were in a semi-detached wooden cabin, deep within a pine forest that had a dry soil road running through its centre, giving it a similar resemblance to a Centre Parks. No traffic went between the cabins except a small bin lorry and a small maintenance van on rare occasions. Directly across from us was another duplicate row of cabins which were a mirror image of our own dwellings. The cabins were small and not much bigger than the type of summer house that you'd see at the end of some wealthy gardens. It had a spacious veranda that reminded me of the type you see with hillbillies sitting in a rocking chair with a couple of blood hound at their feet. The inside was compact in every way, there wasn't enough room to swing a suitcase. A small bedroom with two single beds on the ground floor was ideal for the two boys, while my wife and I had to climb up a ladder each night to reach a loft style double bed. There was also a dining area which was basic in the broadest sense, containing nothing more than a two ring cooker and a sink. It mattered little as this was our new home for the next seven days and we hadn't expected luxury. This little house on the Spanish prairie was all we needed along with two pools and a well-stocked bar only a five-minute walk away, it was ideal for a young family. The following morning, we explored our immediate surroundings and made sure the boys were familiar with some of the new rules. No leaving the front area of the cabin. Don't talk to strangers. No playing out, without sun cream. No taking off your tee shirt or your hat. The list was endless, but it mostly fell on deaf sun-creamed ears. We knew that the first port of call was to be the onsite supermarket for supplies. Water and enough groceries to last seven days was our number one priority. The conversation in the supermacardo was made up of the same stupid observations that every Brit had made before us. 'Oh my god they've got Heinz beans in here and Tomato soup. What flavour crisps do you think these are and do you think their ham is like our ham?' With a basket full of home from home British food, French fries, pizza, Edam cheese, Brazilian coffee and Oreo biscuits, it was time for 'deal or no deal,' at the till. 'Dos mil pesetas por favor' says the girl from Madrid university who is working her way around Spain. 'Si, bueno,' I reply wondering if just for one tiny second, she thinks I'm Spanish too. My wife opens her purse which displays our entire holiday fund bursting at the seams. It opens like a concertina to reveal a wad of paper money and it may never close again, unless we stand on it to realign the zip. I take out a crisp new note that is adorned with what seems to be too many zeros across the front and rear. I examine it briefly before nonchalantly handing it over to the gum chewing senorita. Printed on the note i see the proud face of a man who by all accounts was Hernan Cortez a Spanish conquistador. 'No no no, dos, dos,' the young lady sweeps one hand across her oily black hair and adjusts her ponytail before holding up two fingers to my confused face. 'Ah, dos, si, si, perdon,' I say with a crimson red face that hasn't even had chance to wrinkle in the sun. I panic and pull out a wedge of fresh crisp notes from one of the inner sleeves of the purse and make a fan that would have made a magician proud and hold it like a card trick to her frustrated face. The senorita now looks like she could break out into a flamenco as she stares over the edge of the notes at my incompetent face. She mutters under her breath as she carefully picks out another thousand pesetas from between my fingers. She placed some loose coins back into my hand and I sheepishly thanked her, trying not to annoy her any further. Instead of wondering if she'd charged me the right amount of money, I couldn't help but wonder what slanderous remark she'd made when she'd rattled her well filed fingernails around the drawers of the till. 'English dick head, fucking foreigners,' or perhaps, she said, 'poor guy needs to learn our money and language quickly.'

We should not think badly of our European neighbours, they have a lot to put up with by our presence. Europeans generally visit the UK to see our majestic stately homes and our medieval castles and to experience our dynamic culture. Our history is awash with resplendent characters who not only changed the shape of our country but often the entire world. We in return send our young keen minds to vomit all over the historic streets of Magaluf and Ibiza. We also ship out our older generation to eat, drink and break a hip in Barcelona. We go abroad to let our hair down, ourselves down and our pants down. Indeed, while those pants are down there's no better time for a tattoo of a dolphin at the base of the spine. This is a 'great idea,' inspired by the beautiful creatures that accompanied the booze cruise earlier that day. It will of course be out of sight for most of the year, having more in common with the Loch Ness monster than it does with an intelligent mammal. By intelligent mammal, I am still talking about the dolphin. The following skin infection will turn this wonderful GSE work of art into a monstrosity. It will scab and flake and eventually erupt into a torturous blister lost beneath the crispy texture of preventable sunburn. After a course of antibiotics, it will transform itself into a new and hideously deformed sea creature that lives in a dark secluded place that rarely comes to the surface in daylight. On the rare occasions when it does get exposed to sunlight or an outing at the local swimming baths, people will struggle to understand why you've got a blob fish tattooed just above your arse. The blob-fish, Psychrolutes Marcidus, is seldom seen and has been voted the world's ugliest creature.

It was good to know the shop assistant hadn't ripped me off, but it took about three more days to appreciate this. That's because I had eventually become familiar with the money and could finally say this note is the equivalent of a pound. I believe that's how many of us convert money on holiday. We buy a beer and say that's around two pounds back home and from that point we are financially astute. If on passing the gift shop one of your kids asks for an inflatable shark for the pool you can quickly calculate its value. One shark is equal to eight beers and a large Tia Maria, according to the hiked-up price tag, therefore making it not the only shark in the vicinity. My wife will take the side of the greasy smiling shopkeeper, Senor Grabbo' and tell you to buy two inflatable sharks, one for each of the boys, because they won't share. 'But he didn't want one,' I protest pointing to the youngest of my two boys. 'Well, you can't buy one without the other,' says my wife, which becomes one of the most familiar phrases for the next fifteen years. Senor Grabbo gleefully overhearing the conversation is already taking the sun-bleached great white off its display hook and pumping up another great white into existence with his left foot. 'Ees big, no?' His raucous irritating laugh echoes around his bazar of flip flops and beach towels. By now Grabbo has each shark under both arms and has a toothy grin that matches the jaws printed on the two inflatables. 'Seeex thousand por favor.' I smile awkwardly knowing that I have no choice but to try and deflate his inflated price. 'Tell you what, I'll give you four thousand for the two, good deal yes?' The pretentious smile quickly disappears from the shopkeeper's face and his two thick bushy eyebrows draw together enhancing his already wrinkled frown. 'No, no, eees seeex thousand no less.' Were both sweating at this point, him from the difficulty of having to haggle with the scouse tight arse in broken English and me from the pain and loss of meeting his rip off prices. The red-faced Spaniard is behaving like Quint in Jaws, announcing his price for the shark, 'six thousand pesetas, for that you get the head the tail the whole damn thing.' There was only going to be one winner in this situation and i begrudgingly handed over the correct money to the shopkeeper. The simple fact is you don't only get bitten by mosquitoes on holiday. To this day I hate gift shops and detest the pure and utter garbage that they offer. The gift shops in the U.K. are even worse than abroad. What is it about a fridge magnet or a bottle opener that appeals to so many people on holiday? Traditional bars of rock with lettering all the way through are bought for friends and relatives back home. This cavity inducing sweetener could crack the teeth of a Tyrannosaurus Rex and will also condemn most humans teeth to extinction, it's called 'Rock,' for a reason. Why on earth would people on holiday use up valuable time browsing through repetitive shelves of Chinese tat, is beyond me? A piece of fur chasing a ball, a yapping puppy, and fake watches, Is this really what people want on holiday? I too am the victim of the looky looky man or is it the lucky lucky man? Either way I'm also guilty of buying the fake Rolex watch and all the other garbage so I shouldn't criticise. I eventually realised that we are all easy targets on holiday and as the saying goes, 'a fool and his holiday money are easily parted.'

Parafrugel was hot and it lived up to expectations. Blue cloudless skies stretched as far as the eye could see in every direction. Lathered in sun cream it was now time to find one of the two pools and begin our holiday in earnest. We managed to find a pool which was no further than a five-minute walk from our little cabin. It was a bland looking rectangle with one side flanked with sun beds where motionless bodies soaked up the welcome rays of sunshine. At the furthest point away from us was the deep end of the pool and the shallow end was notably still too deep for small children. Thankfully adjacent to the shallow end of this pool was a small children's pool. It was no more than twelve inches deep all around and ideal for children who were at an infant age. My wife found a place for us to lay our towels and encouraged our two boys to paddle and get their feet wet. Adjoining the pool area was a large courtyard, that seemed mostly taken up with adults. Behind the area of sun beds was a clean spacious cafeteria selling ice creams and beers along with other delightful treats. Finally, it was our time to kick back and relax.

I was never a great swimmer and in truth staying afloat was something that I found immensely difficult. I can swim, but it takes a lot of effort on my part. I can for some absurd reason snorkel exceedingly well. I think it's because I don't need to have my head out of the water and wearing flippers and a snorkel seem to boost my confidence. During my childhood I had several operations on my ears to fix a mastoid problem. This is quite common in children and can cause acute pain making the ears run with a yellow waxy fluid. The operation to stop the infection is quite invasive and the healing process is long and painful. With a head wrapped in bandages you lie on a pillow, and you realise that it's your ears that take the full brunt of the weight of your head. The one thing I'll always remember was the packing that they put in your ears after the operation to absorb all the blood and yuck. If anybody is old enough to remember the old cassette cartridge with its miles of endless tape, they will understand what the packing looked like. When the doctor started to withdraw this from your ears a few days after the operation it felt like they were pulling your brains out such was the pain.

My parents were advised that I should never be allowed even the slightest amount of water into my ears, since I now only had partial eardrums in place. Water would not dispel from any cavities and would collect and fester-causing very painful ear infections. These painful infections were something I had become accustomed to and suffered on a regular basis. It became natural that swimming was something I generally avoided unless tempted due to searing temperatures. My wife Diane was now horizontal and soaking up the rays of the early afternoon sun. Paul and Adam were wading through the shallow pool and seemed blissfully unaware that we were now in another country. There were no other children to share the pool with and unbeknown to us, there was a larger family pool just around the corner full of kids. We knew from the brochure that it existed, but I think we were simply happy to get to a pool, any pool. With the rising temperature the urge to swim got the better of me and I'd noticed that the large pool was completely deserted. I had imagined a scene where everybody was jumping around the pool throwing beach balls and cheering and shouting with the beach boys music in the background belting out 'good vibrations.' Surprisingly, it was totally the opposite. It was a quiet place for those people who didn't want hundreds of snotty screaming kids running around and ruining their holiday. These people came to relax in silence and listen to Simon and Garfunkel on their Sony Walkman's, whispering , The Sound Of silence.' I told my two boys that daddy was going for a swim in the big pool, and they were not to leave the small pool. They gave me some sort of acknowledgement but at their age it's like asking a puppy not to chew the furniture or chase a ball. My wife remained motionless as I took to the water. I'll swim to the deep end and back to the shallow end and that should be enough exercise for today I thought. It was cool and refreshing and an absolute luxury having the pool to myself. I cut through the water using an awkward breaststroke to the edge of the deep end and hung on to the ledge with wet fingertips waiting to catch my breath before returning back to the shallow end of the pool. Behind me I heard the unmistakable voice of my eldest son shouting desperately to get my attention. 'Dad, dad,' he called out frantically pointing towards the water, 'it's Adam, he's jumped in.' I scanned the surface of the pool with my heart in my mouth. Halfway down the pool I could see a mop of blonde hair floating like a jelly fish on the surface of the water. There was no splashing, or hands above the water. I pushed away from the edge of the pool with a mixture of panic and dread, but adrenaline fuelled determination. I knew time would be a critical factor and I swam as fast as I could. I have never done lifesaving in a pool before, but I'd seen it many times on TV. I lifted Adam so his head protruded out of the water and began swimming backwards to the nearby the edge of the pool. He seemed lifeless and was not making a sound. The physical exertion took its toll, and my energy levels were diminishing by the second. I tried desperately to keep myself afloat as i struggled to lift his listless body onto the side of the pool. My wife was still unaware of the unfolding drama and carried on sleeping blissfully unaware. It seemed that the people sat around the pool were also oblivious to the frantic splashing and commotion. Each attempt to lift Adams body on to the side pushed me further underwater and for some selfish reason I thought about my ears and the inevitable consequences. Ridiculous as that sounds it was an inbuilt fear and only added further to the predicament that was far more important. Eventually and totally exhausted I managed to lift my son out of the water with his legs still dangling over the side. I could see and hear him vomiting and was angry and mystified as to why no one had offered any help. I placed my arm on to the edge of the pool and tried with all my remaining strength to lift myself clear of the water, but I couldn't. I was drained of energy and prayed that someone would come to our aid. I was about to call out for help when I suddenly became far more aware of my situation. My toe had scraped the bottom of the pool and within a split second I knew that there was something wrong about my immense struggle. Still spitting water and half choking I stood up to find that the water level was only just above my waist. Adam had been sick and was just about getting into a sitting position when a man appeared carrying a mop and bucket and looked down at me and said, 'You can yusa this for your boys sick, you shoulda be more careful.' Had he witnessed the whole debacle and stood watching from a distance? Was he wondering if we were playing, and it was me that had caused the near drowning of my son? I still hate swimming pools to this day and never really see their appeal, I much prefer the sea and mixing it with a million other creatures that can sting, poison and eat you.

Going on holiday brings us closer together, not only as a family but also as a nation. We meet people from all the other parts of the UK and because we are abroad, we think that the people we meet are like minded. Why else would a family from Wolverhampton pick the same location as me? They say good morning every day, and the family opposite are from Scotland and waved at us yesterday. Lovely proper British people I convince myself. I woke early one day and sat on our small apartment veranda taking in the peaceful early morning scenery. The sun was warm and gentle and still hours away from its promising burning temperatures. It creates an appetite for life that the central heating back home just can't match. You become more observant and notice people and nature like never before. Someone puts their rubbish out and a squirrel arrives seconds later to pick up any loose scraps. A small bird swoops like a feathered ninja onto a table to inspect the leftovers of last night's gatherings which is still amassed with beer cans and the remnants of crisps and peanuts. Some humans appear from behind a partially opened door to inspect the weather and relay their forecast to those still inside. Like a cuckoo clock they dart in and out as if to double check they hadn't missed anything that may change their opinion. Its eerily quiet until a distant cry of 'do as your told or we're going home,' breaks the silence. I was alerted to the creak of our neighbour's door and watched as a tall thin man made his way on to the adjoining veranda. Aged around thirty , he stood with his hands on his hips and looked at me like he was about to do my portrait. 'Morning,' he said in a drawling southern accent, possibly from Devon or Cornwall I guessed. 'Morning,' I replied politely. 'It's a bootifull day, he said in a long-drawn-out kind of way. 'It is mate,' I replied in a quick scouse fashion. 'You got here yesterday, I noticed, you did indeed?' He was making sentences that already had an answer which made it difficult to respond. 'What you be thinking of it here then, it's a wonderful place, that's the ways I sees it.' I need to point out, that these sentences were coming at me at a vocal speed best described as sedated. This bloke was a human tranquilliser and could put someone to sleep from thirty yards away. It got worse as he decided to give me a few tips of places to visit. Holding his chin and looking like he was trying to solve some algebra, he looked towards the entrance of the complex. 'If you goes out thaaat way,' he said, slowly, pointing to a pathway hidden by some trees not far from our location, 'you'll find a small gate.' I looked in the direction he was pointing at but couldn't really picture any kind off pathway. 'Well that there path you're not seeing, takes you down to.' He suddenly stalled mid-sentence and looked in another direction. 'Or is it that ways, I'm not so sure now. No, it be definitely the other way,' he reassured himself. 'Well down there you will find er.' He paused for an age, and it was killing me. I couldn't wait any longer and interrupted with, 'the other pool?' He shook his head slowly and I watched him take a deep breath. 'No.... no....no...., down there you'll find the, er...... the erm...' Once again, I lacked the discretion not to interrupt and tried to head him off. 'The beach,' I said hopefully. 'No.... no, it's the er.... the pathway to the er, road to Lanfranc,' he dragged this dreary information beyond bearable. This neighbourly relationship was never going to work, I had neither the time nor the patience to have a wholehearted conversation with this well-meaning fellow ever again. Appearing from behind the door to his cabin came a small blonde, woman. also, around thirty years of age who bid me good morning in a strong Scottish accent. 'Dina be standing there ya ninny, the wee berns are knocking seven kindsa shite out of each other.' They say the scouse accent comes across as quickly spoken, but this woman spoke so fast that I could see sparks flying off her tongue. How this odd couple had met was beyond comprehension. I spent the entire holiday questioning their relationship and how it worked. Life throws up many mysteries and how these two people from the opposite ends of the country became a permanent relationship is remarkable. I wanted to know how he'd chatted her up. The wedding vows must have taken an age and if his best man was from a similar DNA, like a brother or a close friend, the speeches must have taken an eternity. Later that evening when the kids were tucked up in bed, we were invited over to the opposite cabin were at least a dozen Scottish folk were sitting outside, soaking up more than just the ambience. They had gathered around two large tables that were covered in bottles of beer and wine. They somehow knew our names too, maybe that's why the call the Scottish 'canny?' The word 'canny,' also popped up a lot in their conversation. 'Lester, Diane, come and join us for a wee dram,' one of their parties called out. We probably felt that as we were facing our own cabin the boys would be perfectly safe. This was long before the sad situation that happened with the McCann's in Portugal. The thing about the Scottish is they don't always like the English and why should they? Too much bad history and most of it caused by the English. But a pissed and merry Scot is a different beast all together. 'See you, you scousers, salt of the fucking earth so y' are.' The statement is endorsed around the table as if Robert the Bruce has just made the proclamation himself. 'Aye, Gregor, fucking right. The crowd of relatives agree in unison. Where aboot in Liverpool are ya from?' it's difficult explaining Skelmersdale to people from other parts of the world and it inevitably either confuses them or disappoints them. It's nearly always the same response when you say you're from Liverpool, 'the Beatles,' you know the Beatles?' They say it like they are hoping that you know them personally. The other one is 'you've got a great football team? I'll always remember a voice amongst this party saying something I never expected. 'A canna understand a word the scousers saying, he talks too fucking quickly.' For about an hour I had been second guessing or asking them to repeat what they had been asking me. I'd understood the Senorita behind the supermarket till far better. Our Scottish cousins were more than friendly but after an hour we made our excuses and headed back to our cabin. Later that night the neighbours two doors down decided to have a fist fight worthy of anything shown at Madison Square Gardens and they boxed each other beyond their veranda at two in the morning. Somehow, my wife became the referee and managed to calm the situation down after a lot of risky interventions. The site Security had also turned up but didn't want to become involved and stood back while I did my best to diffuse the situation. My wife took the couple's two children into our cabin and only handed them back when assurances were made of their safety and guarantees to the end of their argument. The next morning the woman who had been physically assaulted by her husband walked past our cabin and smiled at my wife sporting a huge black eye. Id grown up in a similar environment and it didn't shock me as much as it should, even abusers take their family on holiday.

The British are a race made up of so many dialects and accents that contain so many slang words that even their own fellow countrymen don't understand some of the phrases used. Throw together, the Scots, the Irish and the Welsh into one room. Invite the Geordies, Brummies, Scousers and cockneys in to the same room. Add a few Cornish men, some Lancashire folk and you now have a room that can hardly converse in the same language. What's more, you will have a perfect recipe for civil war and blood splattered walls that no one will know how or why it started. British history can be defined by the fact that if we are not at war abroad then we are at war with each other. This sceptred isle as Shakespeare once called it has been divided since the day it became inhabited. The list of wars that have taken place on the fields of the 'not so' United Kingdom are countless, we seem genetically engineered to fight our own neighbours over land, religion and the height of a back garden tree.

Thankfully our Costa Bravado holiday passed without any further incidents and when we arrived home my partner, now wife decided we should get married. I got down on one knee and proposed to her thirty years later in Tenerife.

CHAPTER 2

A Tunisian Honeymoon

The bride and groom took to the floor and danced cheek to cheek in front of their audience. They waltzed slowly to the romantic tones of Lionel Richie's 'Hello.' The evening was now drawing to a close and she whispered gently into his ear, we're going to Tunisia tomorrow.' This was a little strange as to my knowledge there was no money left in the pot. Money was always tight in our house; the sofa had been tipped over a thousand times looking for loose change. Our wedding, was not exactly lavish but it still had all the right ingredients, a traditional church with a choir, white limo's, and a wonderful reception. The first church we'd booked had been struck by lightning and the roof had been completely destroyed. Either me or the vicar was getting a message from high above and we quickly re arranged the venue. The actual day of our wedding had all gone to plan, and not even a little rain could dampen this perfect day. 'Tunisia,' I said looking incredibly surprised at my new wife. 'Yes, it's all paid for, flights, hotel and transfers,' she replied. Diane always gave a calm reassurance even in the bleakest of situations. She does this very well and it's been part of her make up ever since we met and continued right through our marriage. 'Yes, we leave in the morning, kids are staying with your mum for the week, and I've packed our suitcases and passports. There's only one problem,' she said looking beautiful but apprehensive. 'We've got no spending money.' Have you ever noticed how the scratching of an old vinyl record is used to show that something terrible has just happened, this was one of those moments? Lionel Richie's voice faded, and I probably had a vision of Edward Munch's painting 'The Scream,' somewhere in my mind. If they'd have changed our wedding song to 'I just died in your arms tonight,' by the 'cutting crew,' it would not have felt out of place. It turned out that we were fortunate enough to receive some generous donations of cash from our senior family members and by the time we set off for a night in the Red Lion hotel we were no longer in a financial crisis. In 1989 the television had been showing an advert with swim up bars and golden sands with the catch line 'in your dreams you've been to Tunisia.' I wasn't even sure where Tunisia was. I didn't know it was in North Africa and neighboured with Libya and Algeria. It suffered an infamous beach shooting in 2015 which took the lives of thirty-eight people, most of them British. When we landed at Tunis airport all those years ago it was the first time, we had ever seen people carrying a gun. Both the military and the police shared the honours of guarding the airport and they did it without a smile. We were greeted by a tour rep at the airport and guided to a waiting coach that was to take us to our destination. Hammamet is a town situated forty-seven miles from the capital and it takes about two hours by coach to get there. Although a relatively short distance back in 1989 there were no major motorway's to take a direct route to the resort. The coach travelled across a variation of winding roads that passed through small towns and elevated villages. The vast majority of holiday destinations, usually involve another long and often laborious journey from the airport and Hammamet was no exception. I always try to look at the transfer as a perk, a free sight-seeing tour of wherever I'm visiting. Tunisia was like nothing I'd seen before. Many people were dressed in long all in one coveralls called jebbas and the majority of women's faces were hidden or partially veiled. The buildings were either whitewashed or a sandy brown colour and many were in poor condition or in a state of disrepair. Our modern comfortable coach worked its way carefully through the busy narrow streets before joining long stretches of recently built dual carriageways.

It became quickly apparent that the culture beyond my window did not resemble the happy smiling guy in a fez holding a tray of drinks like the one I'd seen on the television. It was strictly hustle and bustle in every direction. Scooters where overburdened with anything from a whole family to a man carrying a kitchen sink. They speedily and skilfully weaved their way past preoccupied pedestrians who didn't seem to notice or even care. Children were running around excitedly between partly constructed market stalls chased by barking dogs that seemed to understand the rules of the games they were playing. Elderly people sat on the edges of the roadside raising their hands to the air as if in prayer and mouthing toothless words in the same direction. We must have looked like a futuristic spaceship carrying aliens from another world peering out and studying the humans below. It wasn't long before I noticed something rather bizarre that was repeated each time we passed through another small village. I was somewhat shocked to see the body of a large animal suspended from its neck by a thick silver chain and positioned a couple of feet to the side of a shop doorway. It became a familiar sight as we worked our way through more streets and more towns, and I eventually became aware that it was a bull's head staring lifelessly at the ground below. This once powerful creature had no expression, it was no longer of this world, and its actuality mattered little. It somehow resembled a person sulking with its chin on its chest not wanting to gaze up at its tormentors. Its dark fleece glistened as it baked painlessly under the hot midday sun, and I could see two large holes on the crown of its head where two magnificent horns would have once protruded. From its neck down the outer carcass appeared to have been cut open as if by a surgeon's scalpel and its outer skin folded behind its back, exposing a mass of internal organs. It looked as if it had been turned inside out and the exposed contents had been varnished to protect it from the blistering heat and humidity. Entrails hung like a jelly fish's tentacles stretching downwards as if desperately trying to touch the floor. Sinews of ruddy brown flesh twisted between blotchy pink intestines resembling those balloon animals that clowns make at a children's birthday party. What was the reason for this macabre display? Initially I guessed it might be a kind of 'help yourself if you can't afford the good cuts of meat.' Or 'hey we are the butchers and were open.' At the time I had no idea of what this signified and it played heavily on my mind. Days later when I had managed to begin a conversation with a local bartender, I took the opportunity to ask him the reason behind the hanging a bull's carcass. I'm not utterly convinced by the answer I received, but it's the only one I ever got. I was told by the bartender at the hotel, that this animal, in-fact any large animal, was hung outside the butcher's premises to keep the flies from landing on the good meat inside the shop. To be honest, it could have been true as flies were plentiful in Tunisia. I sincerely believe that other flies go to Tunisia for a holiday. Tunisia doesn't have big fat bluebottles like we have in the UK, they possess the small and ultra-athletic lightening fly. Much smaller in size when compared to our common housefly, they are highly organised and impossible to catch. They work together like a fighter squadron; indeed, they are the 'Red Arrows' of the insect world.

The hotels plastic sun beds were about as comfortable as a medieval dungeon rack and were the equivalent of an airport runway to a Tunisian fly. While soaking up the blissful rays of November sunshine the only reason to move was to swat these irritable little bastards. The ironic thing , if you kill one there's another billion to take its place. All this pales into insignificance when taking your evening shower. That fuzzy warm feeling of lying in the afternoon sun and sipping a pina colada is quickly forgotten when the cold water suddenly feels like volcanic lava being poured down your back. November in Tunisia is nowhere near the hottest month, but it can still do some damage especially if you were to fall asleep for any length of time. The sun feels deceptively cooler, due to the sea breeze which helps to keep temperatures at a pleasant level. A couple of days into our honeymoon I was tapped on the shoulder by a bloke who had quietly approached our sunbeds, unsure if my wife and I were asleep. Diane was blissfully unaware of his presence as he kneeled down next to me and quietly asked me if I played football. I told him I did, and he asked if I'd like to join a team of other players who were taking on the locals and did, I have any trainers? I mentioned that i had some in my room and would be glad to have a 'kick around.' He explained that it was a regular occurrence with a referee, linesman and they provided a full kit. He asked me to meet him at the reception in fifteen minutes. On reflection I suppose this would have been a good time for me to wake my wife and explain where I was going. But I also thought I'm only going to be an hour on some rough ground at the back of the hotel, so why disturb her? The reception was busy with a crowd of newly acquired players, along with a few extra helpers who worked at the hotel.

The extra helpers were distributing the kit and asking who could play in what position. There was something exciting about this spontaneous international and I quickly became caught up in the atmosphere. 'I play left wing,' I told the self-imposed manager, who was instantly delighted to have a left footer in the team. Before I knew it, I was handed a shirt and shorts along with some clean football socks rolled into a ball and told to get changed in the reception toilets. As I entered the toilets there were other players getting changed and it was easy to strike up conversation. 'We're you from?' asked a tall guy pulling on his shirt. 'Liverpool, 'I replied. 'Scouser in the team, watch your gear. I'm jack and he's Steve, both from Burnley,' no one gets past us,' they both laughed in unison. I found out later they lived up to their word. As we made our way back to the reception, we were given a clipboard and pen and asked to sign something along the lines of 'own risk,' The self-appointed manager was clapping loudly to get our attention and pointed towards the reception doors. Right lads the coach is waiting outside,' Parked directly outside the hotel entrance was a coach similar to the one that we had arrived on. 'All aboard,' came another shout and duly one by one we climbed the stairs without question. I felt a bit like

Pinocchio when he was tempted by Lampwick to go to Pleasure Island. I moved to the back of the coach carrying my loose bundle of clothes and found a seat amongst the many vacant spaces. It was at this point I felt an awful pang of guilt. I'd left my wife behind and disappeared without her knowledge, but I kept telling myself I wouldn't be gone too long. I was wrong, it took just under an hour to arrive at the place we were that match as being held. It turned out to be the most remarkable venue for a football match I'd ever seen. In the U.K. there are some famous dwellings known locally as the bull ring. These notorious blocks of flats built in the sixties are designed in a circular fashion and were given little thought when it came down to aesthetics. I was now standing in the Tunisian equivalent. This was a town somewhere far from the luxury and safety of our four-star hotel. We stood collectively in the centre of a mini colosseum that just happened to have a well-kept football pitch within its grounds. We played under intense pressure as many of the locals hung out from their windows shouting support for their boys and generally making undesirable sounds each time, we touched the ball. I scored that day, and we won by a good margin, but something strange happened just moments after I'd scored. I looked up at the people in the windows in defiant gesture and what followed is something I will never forget .

I could see lots of smiling faces and they were looking at me and shouting 'Liverpool,' in a slow but respectful way. 'Leeeverpoool.' I felt like a gladiator who'd won over his audience because they somehow knew me. Even the other lads looked at me with a quizzical glance as if to say, how do they know? Perhaps I should have shouted, 'no Everton, do i not entertain you?' I've learned it takes too long to explain that there are two great footballing teams in the city of Liverpool. On the return journey back to the hotel, i contemplated how i was going to explain my absence to my wife. I was astonished that Diane didn't go ballistic regarding my away day and as I recall she was quite calm about my disappearing act. I'm sure there would be many a husband in the dog house had they have done what I had done, but I got away with it.

Somewhere in the middle of our holiday we took a coach trip to the Tunisian capital, Tunis and spent some time in the Roman ruins of Carthage. Considered by many as the best Roman ruins outside of Rome. Later in the afternoon we made our way into the centre of the city to walk mainly around the shops and bazars. . The shopping areas in the city are known as medinas which are made up of a labyrinth of dark sloping street that seemed to lead into an abyss. Every avenue sold the same handmade carpets, spices and tourist trash. There were hundreds of bazaars each of them crammed with traditional ornaments, but not a single fridge magnet. It was here we learnt the art of bartering and also realised that beggars truly existed. Back home people didn't sit in the streets outside shops asking for money and yet here it was perfectly acceptable. To see this was a shock to the system and it could have been defined as a wakeup call to how different our life was back home. Roll forward thirty years and we now see people, not just homeless people, begging for money outside almost every shop that has high foot fall. Foodbanks are now common place across the UK and many people can't afford to heat their homes. The great divide has now shrunk between countries and as we move more and more into a cashless society the cups of the poor are now running increasingly dry. The air quality of the Tunis capitol was stifling, and every street seemed to be smothered in a layer of acrid grey smoke that hung like an early morning mist across a Scottish loch. Except this drifting mass meandered like a grey ghost between the traffic and choked the lungs of the city and everyone in it. Most people seemed to accept this cauldron of pollution and for them it seemed perfectly acceptable. The stark difference between our own country and this small but unique corner of Africa was all too apparent. Ashamedly I was more than happy to return to our four-star hotel and had no choice but to turn a blind eye to the corrugated tin shacks that some people called home. The poverty should not have come as a surprise having been told that a polo mint or a cigarette was considered as a good tip for a waiter at the hotel. I was also reliably informed that a full packet of twenty cigarettes would guarantee exceptional service for the whole holiday. A bottle of whisky could be sold for three times its value to the hotel manager or head bartender, and I witnessed this very transaction on the first day of our arrival. Mealtimes at the hotel were not for the faint hearted and it certainly wasn't something to look forward to. The quality of food was extremely poor, although I had a feeling that this was considered as their best cuisine for European tastes. I've never considered myself a fussy eater but the menu at the Hotel Sapphire was remarkably bland. 'Whole fish' fried in oil was to be my first mistake followed by some other culinary disasters that would have caused a prison riot back home. The restaurant was clean and decorated to a high standard and we were allocated a table that was to be ours for the duration of the holiday. We shared this table most evenings with two-night club bouncers from Blackpool who were on a photography vacation. They were a decent pair of blokes who kept us engaged with amusing tales of their duties at the nightclub they both worked at . They weren't built like you'd expect, and you wouldn't have taken them for door attendants. As well as both owning a good sense of humour, they told us that they were keen photographers. They'd arrived in Tunisia a few days earlier and told us of how they'd taken a small train to the location where part of the Star Wars movie had been filmed. Tozeur is in a remote area of the jubilee national park which is mostly Tunisian dessert. They had travelled by rail on an old rickety train through the barren landscape stopping at a few desolate stations along the way. At one particular stop a large crowd of villagers had amassed who started to throw stones at the train, smashing all of the carriage windows and injuring some of the passengers. They were later informed that those responsible for stoning the train believed that the tourists were bringing bad luck with them.

One evening during our honeymoon we were treated to a candle lit dinner, and we were allotted a new dining time and a table to ourselves. As we settled down to our romantically furnished table the two friendly bouncers approached us sheepishly and pleaded to join us. They had been given their own separate table with the same candles and rose petals. I didn't understand why they simply didn't ask for the decorations to be removed. Perhaps sitting together in front of lots of other couples made them feel a bit awkward. So, we ended up sharing our romantic honeymoon meal with a couple of Blackpool doormen. During the meal they mentioned how they'd seen lots of people from the hotel taking a camel ride down near the beach and said it looked to be a lot of fun and we should give it a try.

Never one for sitting still too long, my wife thought it would be a great idea for us to take this camel ride the very next day. Located not far from the hotel beach we managed to find the caravan of camels as described, with their owner trying to entice all those who walked by. It wasn't long before we joined a group of around twenty paying customers and climbed separately onto these slobbering ships of the dessert. There were howls of nervous laughter as people slid awkwardly from side to side trying to gain some sort of balance atop of these ancient modes of transport. I hated it from the word go.

I found myself slipping helplessly towards the back end of my camel and looked at the other riders sheepishly as I found myself in a compromising position. If the camel wasn't worried, i certainly was, because this was not what either of us had signed up for. With a worrying firm hand from the camel driver, I managed to get seated more stably and now looked like a cross between 'Lawrence of Arabia' and 'The Hunchback of Notre Dame.' The owner of the camels gave a loud command and they collectively started lurching forward in unison. Again, this brought about further outbursts of laughter as we set off to a distant patch of rough ground away from the beach. We plodded along smiling and waving to onlookers and eventually settled into the unusual motion that comes with riding a camel. You soon realise that you must work with the camel and be prepared to be as flexible as possible. Perhaps this is how the concept of belly dancing originated as you wobble uncontrollably like blob of jelly on a spoon. After about fifteen minutes we reached an area of scrub land that had a large proportion of small thin trees bordering the edge of some dry gravel pathways. As we headed somewhat purposely into the direction of this featureless wilderness, I noticed the owner who was riding a battered old 1960's moped disappear in the opposite direction. These camels obviously know the routine I thought, after all they must have done this journey a thousand times. However, it did concern me that the camel driver wasn't actually driving and had buggered off leaving a trail of dust in his wake. Everybody was now over the initial excitement of riding a camel and was now relaxed enough to take in the views. I too felt that my angst towards camel riding had now subsided even though I was still sitting slightly lobsided. I found myself less nervous and began to relax giving the occasional smile and wave to my wife who was now some distance in front of me. Then without warning all hell broke loose and my camel suddenly went fucking rogue. It must have been harbouring an escape plan and had decided on this day of all days it was time to put it into action. This was one clever camel; it knew exactly when the camel driver would piss off for a coffee. It had also figured out, that if it broke out into the slightest run that he could shake this amateur jockey off his back. How wrong he was, little did he know i was the Llandudno donkey derby champion of 75. I'd also ridden a bucking bronco in a county show, so i was not going to be shaken off that easily. Years of planning had gone into this daring escape and I'm sure the other camels may have considered making the break for freedom with him, but they must have sensibly declined. I watched dumbfounded as the camel train made a gentle right turn and continued down the regular dusty gravel path. Meanwhile the Steve McQueen of the camel world had other aspirations and had turned left breaking into a solid gallop. The great escape was now in full swing. I could just about hear my fellow riders laughing somewhere in the distance behind me, seconds later a glance over my shoulder confirmed they had all disappeared out of sight. My 'ship of the dessert,' was now in full blown mutiny and had picked up the pace. We were somewhere between trotting and running and my shouts of 'woah boy,' were falling on deaf ears. He, I'm presuming it was male, took me headlong through the trees that overhung the path and I found myself breaking small branches as we galloped across the landscape. To my absolute horror we suddenly stopped on the edge of a very steep gulley. From where I was sitting it was like peering down into the Grand Canyon. This camel started lifting its front leg off the ground and stroked the air as if trying to find a step on an invisible ladder. 'What the fuck are you doing?' I don't think he understood English but there was no way I was going to die sitting on the hump of a renegade camel and his bid for freedom. I could see the front of the Daily Mirror newspaper with the headline of 'Man killed by camel in freak accident.' Then some hack making light of the story. '*A honeymoon ended in tragedy when a runaway camel named Addawser took the hump and hurled itself and its rider off the edge of a cliff this week.*' Thankfully and not a moment too soon the owner and so-called camel driver arrived shouting and screaming over the spluttering of his dilapidated moped. Whatever he was saying must have translated as 'reverse,' and mercifully that's exactly what we did. He slapped Addawser on the arse with a long stick and angrily called out some meaningful words in Arabic. As he scolded his rogue money maker. In return, i scolded the camel driver with a few choice words of my own. 'Where the fuck have you been? This thing is out of control, he could have killed me, I want to get off.' With that he just rode right past me with a gummy smile waving his stick in the air shouting meaningless drivel. A short time later I converged with the rest of the riders, and we made our way back to the beach. Dismounting from a camel is just as difficult as getting on the ugly beast in the first place. Most of us fell off headfirst and stood up with a mouthful of sand. Would i consider riding a camel again, no, never again, not in my lifetime!

When the pain in my backside had finally subsided, we decided to take an evening walk down to the nearby beach. At the edge of the hotel beyond some well-kept gardens there was a gate that opened onto a white sandy beach. The sun was beginning to dip over the horizon, and we were treated to one of those picture postcard settings. The evening sky was an artist's dream, filled with deep red brush strokes and smears of burnt orange. Frantic white horses threw themselves onto the beach before spreading into paper thin layers waiting to be absorbed back into the sand. We lost all track of time jumping the massive waves and finally admitted defeat when it became too dark to continue. We returned to the hotel tired but euphoric at the same time. We changed into some evening clothes and set off to join the other residents in the hotel bar. We had been warned that leaving the hotel after dark was a risk not to be taken lightly. But this rumour was credited to the hotel owners who were ensuring that guests spent their money on site. The hotel bar was limited when it came to choice and there was only one brand of beer along with some creative local spirits. The large function room had become segregated by the two main nationalities, creating an imaginary divide between the British and the Germans. The British residents occupied the side of the room nearest to the bar. The German holiday makers of which there were many, sat directly across the room, deep in conversation. Everything seemed amicable and friendly but that was soon to change. From behind a red velvet curtain that surrounded a very small stage stepped a rather tall guy who had uncontrollable bushy hair that immediately caught your attention. 'Good evening, everybody, tonight is the bingo night, and we have prizes of plentiful free drinks.' His English wasn't great but understandable. Bingo tickets were strewn around the tables so there was no need to purchase in order to play and with no cash prize it would be nothing more than a bit of fun. I was wrong, when the bingo started the entire place fell into a deathly silence. The caller who was Tunisian, wore a gold sequinned jacket that rubber stamped his title of host, entertainer and compare for the evening. Bingo it would seem, is taken very seriously in Germany as much as it is in the U.K. Anyone raising their voice or clinking a glass was immediately met with cold stares from both nations. This amateur Bingo caller hadn't quite grasped the enormity of the game, especially as it was now a matter of national pride. He was struggling with the numbers. I imagined that he'd only just finished some brief training from a UK holiday rep. 'Ok everybody down with the eyes and look up. Your first number eesa clickity six. The next number is a duck for two.' Groans of despair could be heard across the room, and the pace was beyond slow. Finally, the number of balls in the machine were beginning to dwindle. 'Who is waiting for thirty-one,' the caller announced prematurely over the microphone? Someone gave a joyous shout of 'house' and held their card into the air. 'Eeeesa a pity cos theees is thirty-two.' This brought about howls of laughter from all around the room and the novice bingo caller must have thought he had done something that was acceptable. The rest of the game continued in the same vein.

Every night most people exchanged travellers' cheques at the reception for Tunisian Dina's, at a rate of about four Dina's to the pound. We were getting short of money with two nights stay still remaining and worse still we had missed the exchange cut off point. The hotel safe was locked at six every evening and no amount of pleading would open it. We were now resigned to an early night with only enough money to buy one drink each. Our new friends the doormen joined us at our lounge table, and it wasn't long before we were joined by more residents. The conversation as I remember, was like a gathering of old friends who just wanted to have a good laugh and get sloshed. It wasn't long before we had to announce that we were going back to our room due to a lack of funds. The Blackpool bouncers were having none of this and insisted on paying for our drinks for the rest of the evening. When other guests discovered that we were on our honeymoon, complimentary drinks soon filled our table. Our sequinned host had now changed roles from bingo caller to

DJ for the evening. The music he played would be best described as embarrassing old party hits. 'Brown Girl in the ring,' and the 'Birdy Song,' those annoying type of tunes at a children's party. He played the song 'I am the music man,' something you would definitely expect at a kid's party and known to the Germans as 'ich bin ein musikante. The alcohol was beginning to take affect and it was becoming apparent that most people had been drinking steadily throughout the day. As the Germans sang along to the song in their own language the British bulldog started to growl menacingly from the other side of the room. There is a part that mentions playing the trombone in the lyrics to the 'music man,' and the German guests seemed to relish the part that goes 'oomp-pa-pa, oomp-pa-pa,' and stood up in unison to mime the actions of playing a trombone. As the music man reached the part that has the Dam Busters' theme, up stands a group of fat, balding beer bellied brits. Using their arms as wings they begin running towards the Germans who are now retreating behind their tables. Marvellous, just what we needed, a re-enactment of the Second World War and a group of pissed up brits impersonating the 617 squadron. The Germans could see this was going beyond the theme of a party song and most of us looked on with awkward embarrassment. The Mosquito was the name given to the plane flown by these heroic pilots during the second world war. These human mosquitoes were fuelled by alcohol also with a thirst for blood. Thankfully before anyone had the inclination to launch a bouncing bomb the DJ changed the music and quickly jumped down from behind his decks into the aggressive crowd of brits who were repulsively goading the Germans and now leaning menacingly over their tables. The DJ who had inadvertently brought this on with his agitating mega mix was probably thinking either he gets a peace treaty sorted, or he gets the sack for starting a Third World War. He explained to the drunken brits that the Germans were being friendly and were singing along with the British and they should calm down and enjoy the evening. A truce was quickly declared and most of us breathed a sigh of relief. This is why as a nation we are frowned upon abroad as we continue to bombard are European neighbours with these dickheads by the plane load. My wife once asked a savvy Turkish bar owner how he knew the difference between the Germans and English before they'd even entered his bar. She had noticed that he could speak fluently in both languages and greeted his customers in their own language before they'd actually opened their mouths. He replied, most British men were fat, beer bellied, bald and covered with bad tattoos. 'They have a bulldog tattoo somewhere on their leg and tattoos on their necks and very often have a red face and white balding head.' The Germans are more reserved, he admitted, but will take over the bar. They will never queue for anything and can be rude and demanding. Worse still, they have very poor taste in fashion and are easily recognised by their eternal eighties attire. The night continued without a hitch. My wife ended up dancing on the tables, I ended up talking football with some people from Tamworth and everyone made it back to their rooms without anything being 'busted.' The next day was our last day, and we were up early with the customary hangover and still needing to pack. I bundled everything into the suitcase apart from my shoes, which had already been stolen from the room days earlier. We had been given numerous warnings that shoes had a habit of walking off on their own. In some ways I wasn't concerned, if someone was desperate enough to steal a pair of brogues, that's alright with me. Breakfast was of a continental affair with rolls of bread that could have been used in a sling shot to kill Goliath and a coffee that would lubricate a bike chain. By lunch we were down to our last few dina's, and we had just enough money to purchase a pizza. These thin crusty discs were freshly baked in an outside oven close to the pool. By the time our order had arrived at the table, it was covered in flies making it look like we'd asked for black olives as a topping. We were both famished, and my wife was now having second thoughts about eating this gooey Italian fly trap. I picked out at least half a dozen of these kamikaze flies and told my wife to close her eyes. The pizza had arrived already cut into eight triangular pieces and once id removed the offenders, I spun the plate in circles for a few seconds. 'It's pizza Russian roulette,' you don't know which piece had a fly in it, so don't worry.' We devoured the entire pizza in seconds. In fact, the pizzas and the crisps from a small shop in the foyer were the only edible food in the hotel during the whole holiday. We were never entirely sure what flavour the crisps were, but we basically survived the entire week on them. They could have been 'well hung bull,' flavour, for all we knew. On the flight home we were astonished to witness people asking other passengers if they were eating or leaving certain items of food on their trays. Tunisia had built some amazing hotels, but they were not ready to cater for the Europeans. By now I'm sure there's a KFC and a McDonalds taking their proud history into the twentieth century. They had a saying in Tunisia, that if an accident occurs it must have something to blame, not someone.' While taking a taxi to Hammamet, my wife and I noticed how many cars were abandoned in the deep ditches that ran alongside the straight but narrow roads. Sitting on a piece of wooden board which doubled for a seat and with no handles to wind the windows down, we began to question our sanity. We were lucky enough to have a driver who spoke good English and pointed out a few common features along the way. 'Why so many cars in the ditches,' I asked? 'This my friend is because many of our people have no insurance and no matter who caused the accident, no one pays. They say the car was to blame and therefore the car is never recovered and that is that.' I was dumbstruck, how does this work, how can it work, surely someone puts up a fight. Basically, if you get the car recovered you are then admitting you were at fault. Please remember, this was over thirty years ago, so I'm sure things will have certainly changed. Ten minutes further into our journey it became apparent as to why there was so many vehicles abandoned along the roadside. I quickly established that the highway code of Tunisia at this time was completely based on 'chicken.' Once again, another referral to our fine feathered friend.

CHAPTER 3

My Precious

Let's jump ahead to the future rather than move in a chronological order. My wife and I very often travelled abroad for a special occasion. This was usually for a birthday or an anniversary. We decided to take a flight to Paris to celebrate our twenty fifth anniversary and spend a long weekend visiting some of the iconic sights. We stayed at a small hotel which was within easy walking distance to the Arc de Triomph. I don't recall the details of the hotel except it was chic and clean. This is a priority when living with someone who in my opinion is bordering on OCD regarding cleanliness. My wife would probably deny this and say something along the lines of, 'you wouldn't like it if I was dirty, would you?' To which I will say, er, cleanliness is next to godliness. I always remember my daughter taking her own pillow to a Bed and Breakfast that we'd found at the last minute in a seaside town. It wasn't the cleanest of places and sadly the only place remaining that advertised vacancies in the window. After climbing a few flights of sticky stairs, we were shown into a room by a landlady who looked like Gimli the dwarf in Lord Of the Rings, minus the axe. The décor and features of the room were beyond description, but ill try. The wallpaper was nicotine yellow, and the bedding was straight from the barracks of Full Metal jacket or some military academy. The landlady left us with a few instructions regarding breakfast and made her way back down the stairs. My daughter looked at our faces and quipped, 'I'm glad i brought my own pillow so I'm not putting my face against other people's slobber. Ten minutes later we were driving home. Since my daughter made this famous quote, i have taken my pillow to dozens of countries and hotels all over the world.

Thankfully the hotel in Paris was perfect and we wasted little time in setting off for the Arc de Triomph, which on good information was close by. The avenue leading away from our hotel was decorated with lines of leafy green trees that kept its residents briefly in touch with nature. Resembling the spokes of a wheel, the avenues of Foch, Hugo and Kleber were all connected to a central hub that completely encompassed the famous landmark. Completed in 1836 the Arc was created to immortalise the armies who fought in the French Revolution and the Napoleonic wars. During the year of 1812, 600,000 soldiers embarked on a conquest of Russia and only ten thousand returned, a catastrophic loss of nearly an entire army.

To get to this famous landmark, would involve using various underpasses and subways that would emerge at the centre of the iconic monument. It would be impossible to actually cross the road due to the endless volume of revolving traffic that continuously beeped their horns at each other which was duly ignored as it was impossible to tell who was at fault. Not even Napoleon would have tried this crossing and he like the rest of us would have no choice but to take to the trenches. As we worked our way in the direction of the Des Champs Elysees, there was a matter of some wide pedestrian crossings to negotiate. Huddled together like a herd of wilder beast, someone would lead the way and step cautiously onto the crossing of the Avenue Marceau. It was strange how so many people crossing from the opposite side of the road don't clash with the other people trying to cross from the other side of the road. Humans have an uncanny way of avoiding each other in densely populated situations. Halfway across the crossing I felt a tap on the shoulder, by a man who i think was from an Arab descent. Not wishing to offend, i am told this is the correct way to address people from areas such as Lebanon, Iran, Saudi Arabia, etc. This description is quite necessary for me to tell you of how I nearly became hoodwinked by a clever scam that plays on the honesty of the victim. By the time I'd reached the opposite side of the road I had been presented with a gentleman's heavy gold ring. The man who had grabbed me was somewhere in his mid-thirties with short dark curly hair and dressed in smart casual clothes. 'You dropped your wedding ring sir,' he said almost apologetically. 'It came off your finger as you were crossing, I picked it up.' He smiled and held it in a manner that ensured I could appreciate its proportions. An experienced jeweller could probably estimate the price range of this heavy gold ring just by its dimensions. Of course, i appreciated that jewellery needs close evaluation using weight, clarity and other methods of appraisal. Nevertheless, something such as gold automatically implies value to the human eye. Somewhere in my brain in the compartment labelled 'conflict' I heard myself saying, 'take it, just take it.' I resisted temptation and showed him my left hand with my wedding ring still firmly attached to my third finger. 'Oh, in that case you must take it because I will never find the true owner now,' he pointed at people walking in different directions to emphasize his point. How strange that I relaxed my hand just enough for the ring to be placed willingly into my open palm. He looked at me with a knowing smile and closed my fingers gently. 'Take it, it is yours, I am not allowed to wear gold, it is against my religion, it is your lucky day.' I did try, albeit not very hard to make him to take it back, but I suddenly felt the weight of the ring and I lost my voice. 'My precious,' I could hear hissing and smouldering through my mind. 'Precious belongs with you it does,' spoke the voice in my head, 'my precious, is mine, mine i tells you.' I turned and walked away shrugging my shoulders and estimating its weight to be somewhere around 'kerching.' Minutes later the same guy amazingly managed to bump into me again in the middle of another crowd of pedestrians. Paris is possibly smaller than it looks. 'Oh, we meet again my friend,' he said greeting me like we'd gone to the same school. I was thinking perhaps you can give me twenty euros for some food and coffee, then both of us will have had a good day, yes?' The lord of the fake rings had come to claim his reward and I for one was not fooled for a minute. This only confirmed what I'd already known, I was carrying a lump of shiny brass in my pocket. I told him to take it back, but he refused and kicked up a fuss. Eventually when he realised that there was not a chance of me parting with any cash whatsoever, he took off in another direction swearing and waving his arms furiously. I kept the ring for over twenty years as a constant reminder of how easy it was to be the victim of a holiday scam. I lost the ring some years later and therefore lost its powers to protect me from being duped again.

Paris was everything we'd expected and more. We dashed about at breakneck speed in order to try and take in as many of the capital's main attractions as possible. A trip down the river Seine past Notre Dame was far better than I had imagined. The view from the barge is well worth the fare alone and as you glide eloquently past the riverside bars and restaurants it gives you a flavour of Paris like no other. The walk across the Pont d Lena bridge which connects the Eiffel Tower to the Fountains de Trocadero is notably weighed down with thousands of padlocks, attached by lovers to the already heavy black chains. A strange custom possibly developed by a locksmith, which I've noticed is now popular in many other countries too. I also happened to notice a sign printed in English and French at the opening to the bridge stating. *'Due to the increasing weight and stress that has been added to the bridge from padlocks, we will be removing and replacing the chains for safety reasons.'* When it comes to cutting things off the French are somewhat renowned. Channel tunnels, channel ferries and heads of royalty, have all been cut off with scant disregard. The French are very adept at holding its own country and ours to ransom. By blocking access to the channel tunnel and the northern ports it can close our trade lanes very quickly. This has an impact on both the UK and France and the French government usually caves into whatever demands are being requested. Famous for its use of the guillotine, the French adopted the famous device created by Dr

Joseph-Ignace Guillotin, to serve justice to those it believed to be guilty of various crimes. During the French revolution it worked overtime to reduce and behead its aristocracy. This period of history catches everybody's imagination and that's mainly due to the names of those who ended up beneath its oblique blade. Probably remembered for taking the head of king Louis XVI and his queen Marie Antoinette more so than any other of its other victims. The implementation of the guillotine was to make death as quick and as painless as possible; this was because other methods of beheading had often relied on the accuracy of some big brute with an axe. Decapitation as a method of punishment seems to have been very popular for hundreds of years but it was often a bloody and messy affair. Even British royalty were not spared from a hacking job when it came to losing their heads. It is reported that it took the executioner three swings to help Mary Queen of Scots part with her head.

On our second day in Paris, we were greeted with a cloudless blue sky. The early morning sunshine brought a warmth that sent a vibe throughout the busy city streets. We wasted no time in executing our plans and set off on foot to the nearest railway station. Clutching two return tickets to Versailles we were full of giddy anticipation. Okay in truth, out of the two of us I'm the history geek, so i was the one who was giddy not my wife. The palace reeks of opulence and is situated just fifteen miles outside the city boundaries. As you walk up the gentle slope towards the gold and black gates it becomes all too easy to understand why the common people of Paris filed a complaint. We're talking extravagance beyond compare. The architecture and elegance have been quoted as costing in today's money at somewhere in the region of 300 billion dollars and all paid for by le froggy taxpayer. The poor people of the French Republic were starving and quite rightly 'pissed off.' They didn't have food banks to fall back on like they do in modern Britain today. Basically, those in power were putting up gold wallpaper while starving people where actually eating paper. Seems Boris Johnson should have considered this during his own renovations whilst in power.

Although hardly comparable, the residents of number ten will eventually always get the chop for poor judgement. Versailles is a place that should figure highly on your bucket list if you have one. It shows that the hand that feeds you will drag you to the gallows if necessary. Yes, the palace may have cost an arm and a leg and a few heads along the way, but it's truly a magnificent salute to opulence. Not only will you see all the finery and riches that you would associate with the interior of a palace, but you will also be amazed by the magnificent, landscaped gardens. Large pools containing spectacular fountains have been designed with white marble statues of Greek gods and animals as their centre piece. The cost of producing this grandiose building went far beyond the accumulated wealth of the French royal family. When the people of Paris became so destitute and dying of starvation there was only going to be one outcome. They revolted and famously disposed of their Royal family otherwise known as the house of Bourbon. Snails, frogs' legs and bread were soon back on the menu, and even the occasional cake. The French peasantry soon made up for lost time and grew into a bustling city of wealthy merchants. Later in the afternoon we boarded another train that took us back into the heart of Paris. The natural daylight was now fading quickly and by the time we arrived back in the city a different atmosphere had now taken the place of the brisk morning sunshine we had left behind earlier. Instead of heading back to the hotel, we had made the decision to head towards the Eiffel tower. Like a pair of moths, we'd been attracted by the impressive light show which had started to illuminate and decorate the whole tower from top to bottom. The dancing shapes and colours were certainly impressive, but it seemed to degrade this iconic structure and it felt more in keeping with Blackpool than Paris. The crowds that gathered below the towers solid steel legs, danced to the various busker's music while taking photographs and selfie's which created an impromptu party atmosphere. After about an hour or so, we made our way back across the Pont d' l'ena bridge along a road by the name of Avenue Kleber. Thirsty and hungry we found ourselves entering a bar by the name of Frog XVI and here we spent the rest of the evening dining and chatting about the day's events. It was the first time I'd seen or heard of a 'micro-brewery,' which was fascinating in its concept and caught on in the UK some years later. While sitting in a comfortable booth i found myself staring down at the huge highly polished copper vats that were creating the very drink that I was holding. Lost in the ambience of one of the most romantic cities in the world, It soon felt like I'd polished off the contents of one of those vats on my own. When, as is always the case, my wife says it's time to go, I made my way to the bar to pay the tab. When presented with the bill i immediately noted the total and passed it back to the bar tender. 'That's not mine,' I said innocently. Expecting a reply of, 'I beg zee pardon monsieur, I av given you ze party of douze in error.' But he pushed the bill back towards me. 'La table dix neuf is sixty euros, ees for you we, we.' We we, was close, but in truth poo poo would be closer, I nearly shit myself. Was this guy building a new palace? It seemed that the French revolution was still in full swing, and this new establishment was out to make a killing. I paid, resentfully, and with a bit of support from the wife i wobbled my way back to the hotel. My lack of balance may have been due to the shock or a little tiredness. In the morning, my head felt like I'd been whacked by Queen Mary's crap executioner. A little later and a little more sober i realised that 'Paris maybe lovely in the springtime,' as mentioned in the Cole porter song, but it sure is expensive!

CHAPTER 4

Stella Fella

I've been to Lanzarote so many times I've genuinely lost count. One particular trip to Lanzarote was with my brother and his wife and my niece aged four. We had chosen to fly from Liverpool's Speke airport to Arricife, Lanzarote. The early nineties had not seen much cash injection into Liverpool and its airport was still very small and yet to be developed. It wasn't until 2001 that it had some major investment and was renamed to John Lennon airport. In the nineties there were no lines of queuing people or automated boards displaying dozens of flights. This was a traveller's dream with regards to getting through an airport and onto a plane. Passport control was stress free and completely different to the modern-day stressful experience, especially where airport security was concerned. All those families that were on the flight to Arrecife were now gathered in a small area at the end of the airport, and it looked for all the world like a hospital waiting room. Rows of thinly cushioned seats, were bolted to the floor facing in the direction of what looked like a pair of sliding glass doors. The only thing that gave this drab waiting area any appeal was a small bar positioned at the opposite end of the room. The bar was designed to look like a local pub, the kind of place that you'd expect to see a darts board and a pool table. It wasn't too long before me, and my brother had made our excuses to have a catch up over a pint. We were soon joined at the bar by an older man whose appearance took us both by surprise. Small in height and approaching his late sixties, he called out to the bar person for a pint of Stella. We both stared intently at the man now staring back at us and he knew that we were thinking. Around his head was a miniature scaffold. It was a construction of shiny metal bars with intricate screw threads and small adjustable wheels. He looked like 'Pin Head, from the Hell Raiser movie. He picked up his pint with one hand and pointed upwards with the other while looking at me and my brother. 'This? Fractured skull, fell over, pissed.' This was announced quite proudly with a scouse accent that was so thick it would have needed subtitles on television. 'I don't even wanna fuckin go on ollyday, know what a mean like? Me daughters talked me into this. I told dem I wanna go to fucking Cornwall, do a bit a fishing like, know whata mean lads?' This guy was a professional scouser and he was washing down pints of Stella Artois like he'd just walked out of the Sahara dessert. We spent half an hour at the bar with this chap and witnessed how quickly the power of Stella Artois was beginning to consume him. Each time he went to the toilet my brother and I talked about him rapidly. 'Christ, hope we're not sitting next to him on the plane,' my brother said nervously. 'I keep thinking he's going to get that scaffolding on his head tangled up in some protruding obstacle.' We laughed aloud, but we were conscious of his return.

We decided it would be best to return to our families and wait to be called out for the flight. Later we noticed the guy from the bar saunter back to his two daughters and three grandchildren looking decidedly edgy and supporting himself by holding on firmly to a row of chairs. We were flying with a Spanish airline called Futura, which was staffed entirely by a Spanish crew. Speke airport reminded me of something that resembled a Pepper Pig episode, you can tell I've got grandchildren. It was all so simple back then and much less complicated. To our surprise the plane pulled up as close as it could to the large glass doors and within minutes a member of the crew slid open the large glass doors and beckoned us with a wave. The room emptied in an orderly manner, and we made our way outside to ascend the mobile flight of stairs that were propped against the aircraft door. As mentioned earlier, when taking my seat my immediate priority is to go through a mental checklist. Nearest door, check, suspicious looking passengers, all look good apart from Pin head, check, does the crew look competent, check? Dodgy old scouser, shit, opposite isle to us, shit. As the pilot and crew prepared us for take-off, I began to take an interest in the layout of the aircraft. There was only one toilet and that was positioned at the very front of the plane left of the cockpit door. To the right of the cockpit door was a small kitchen area that was hidden behind a bright floral curtain. I have never seen anything like this on any other aircraft before or since. I later found out that Futura was founded in 1989 and ceased trading in 2008. Basically, we were on a plane that should any person need to rush to the toilet, it could be easily mistaken for an attempted hi jacking. Worse still if a queue develops there could be a lot of river dancing as one toilet between two hundred or more people is a recipe for disaster. What if the pilot needs to go to the toilet, does he have to go the back of the queue like everybody else? It didn't sit comfortably with me, thinking that the pilot will be standing behind ten people in a queue for the toilet. My fear of flying starts to consume me and i have to find a distraction to stop me analysing and fearing the worst. However, the take off into the Liverpool skies was silky smooth and very reassuring, so my time scrutinising and risk calculating was wasted, a bit like the guy with the scaffolding on his head. After around fifteen to twenty minutes, the seat belt sign was turned off, signalling the fact that we had now levelled out. A familiar voice suddenly called out over the hum of the engines from the line of seats opposite. 'Thank fuck for that, I'm going for a piss,' announced the owner of a slurred scouse accent who was now hauling himself towards the empty isle. Before he'd made his decision to set off for the distant toilet, I'd noticed a few minutes earlier that the cockpit door had opened, and the pilot had shimmied behind the kitchen curtain. Pin head was now using every chair as a support mechanism to get him to the front of the plane. Most of the isle passengers gave him a glaring look as he clumsily gripped each headrest and fell from side to side. As his seat was situated towards the rear of the plane, it was quite a journey to reach the one and only toilet. Of course, it was guaranteed that he'd be the first person to make a dash for the toilet, his bladder must have been on the verge of bursting like a water balloon. Just as he got to the front of the plane another person stood up in front of him with the same intention. He now had to wait his turn and he stood staring back at the passengers looking extremely uncomfortable and rather bizarre. He looked like a caged pit bull terrier, bearing his teeth in an impatient snarl. The plane gave a small jolt, nothing that would be remotely classed as turbulence but just enough to swing open the cockpit door. The door inadvertently touched his back and therefore caught his attention. Desperately waiting to relieve himself he turned around to face what he must have thought was the touch of a person. He was now staring through the half open door of the cockpit at an empty chair where the pilot should have been sitting. Through the flight deck windows he would now have the view that was reserved for someone who has trained meticulously for many years. His line of sight didn't allow him a complete view of the whole cockpit so he would not have seen the co-pilot. In an alcohol fuelled frenzy he was about to raise hell. (As i said 'Pin Head, Hell Raiser see the way i stitched that together?) He turned around to face the rows of calmly seated passengers, eyes glazed with fear and screamed, 'oh my god, there's no one flying the fucking plane!'

He was pointing into the cockpit and looking at us like he was preaching a sermon with all the vigour of those preachers you see in the Southern states of America. The curtain which was now positioned to the man's left-hand side flew back very quickly, were upon a steward and flight attendant came out to confront him. The pilot squeezed behind him to get back into the flight deck closing the door securely behind him. The flight attendant grabbed the man by his arm and insisted he return to his seat. She was then joined by another flight attendant from the back of the plane who tried to calm the situation but to no avail and therefore decided to get physical. I was dumbstruck when I watched the flight attendant grab this guy's surgical frame and pulled him down the aisle like a farmer holding the nose ring of a bull. He complained bitterly as he was forcibly taken to his seat and was threatened with police action. The flight attendant then warned him in broken English, that if he left his chair one more time, he would be handed to airport security when we landed. His own daughters pleaded with him to calm down and in thankfully he became subdued by their desperate pleading. I heard him call out a few times that he needed 'a piss,' but he never left his chair for the remainder of the journey. How he managed to hold on is a miracle, credit where its due I certainly couldn't have held on for another four hours. After we had landed and people gathered outside the various coach stops to take them to their hotel, all eyes were upon this man and his family. Everybody would have been thinking the same thing, 'not my coach, not my hotel, please god.'

Family and relatives don't always make the best companions, and it can bring relationships very close to breaking point. There are reasons why most of us live in separate towns and cities to our siblings. As children we argued who was having the crust on the bread or the biggest piece of cake. We fought for attention and stole each other's favourite belongings. As the saying goes, 'you can choose your friends, but you can't choose your family and a family holiday can endorse this saying all the more. You will become aware of the subtle things that have set you apart and you will suddenly realise, that being from the same parents doesn't necessarily mean your DNA plays the same tune. During this holiday, my brother who reminds me of the comedian Jack Dee, fell for a scratch card scam and believed that he had won a camcorder. To be fair a camcorder was an expensive item and a desirable piece of electronics back then especially for free. The main boulevard of Puerto Del Carmen is usually crammed with people taking a stroll to the beach or browsing around the many gift shops. It was somewhere between lunchtime and mid-afternoon that we found ourselves heading down the hill with no agenda and probably catch a pint in one of the bars. It was an extremely hot day and we had decided that sitting around the pool in the searing heat may not be such a good idea. While browsing through the customary trinket shops a young lady took the opportunity to approach us and gave all the adults a complimentary scratch card. Surprise, surprise, our scratch cards revealed that we had each won a camcorder and some other goodies. I'd been warned many times by experienced travellers that it was nothing more than a way to get you to visit 'time share,' developments. After explaining this to my brother i was surprised that he was still quite happy to go along to a demonstration in order to collect his expensive prize. I showed no interest and told him it's a scam that's been around for ages, and he'd win another camcorder tomorrow. 'It's your holiday but these people are stealing your time,' i remember telling him feeling older and wiser. He asked the girl if he'd really won a camcorder and she confirmed that he only had to go for a couple of hours to the complex and he would be able to claim his free gift. I refused to go, and I threw my prize-winning scratch card in the bin and waved them goodbye as they got in a van. It crazy how we allow ourselves to be kidnapped without a struggle and to get in a vehicle voluntarily with our children, yet we tell our children not to talk or go anywhere with strangers. Hours later I started to get slightly concerned that my brother's hadn't returned along with his wife and four-year-old daughter. I kept looking towards the entrance to our complex thinking surely, they would have been dropped off at the hotel and not back at the place where they had been picked up?

When they finally appeared, it turned out they had mistakenly been dropped off at the wrong hotel, my brother, his wife and daughter had ended up walking at least two miles. They looked exhausted as they walked through the complex and i could see he was not looking too pleased. I stood up and went to the edge of the pool, 'film me diving in the pool,' I shouted, to which he shook his head, gave me a v sign and walked straight towards his room.

A day or two later i told my brother that the best way to see the island was to hire a car. He was slightly nervous as he hadn't driven abroad before, but i assured him it wasn't too difficult.

This is something I'd done a couple of times on other holidays to Lanzarote, so i was quietly confident that my brother would enjoy the same experience. Unfortunately, my brother didn't get off to a good start and i can only imagine the stress he must have gone through. After we had both signed up and received the keys to our hire cars, I told my brother to follow me back up the hill to our hotel. From my previous experiences of driving around Lanzarote, i was quick to settle into the adaptions needed to drive on the right-hand side of the road. For a brief moment i lost sight of my brother who should have been right behind me, and he somehow failed to show up at the hotel. After two hours had passed and a fruitless search back to the car hire place, he finally pulled into the hotel car park. He began to explain where he had been, and how he'd lost sight of me due to giving way to another car and subsequently took a wrong turn. He had by some bizarre misfortune made his way into Arricife which is the capitol of Lanzarote. With its busy roads and heavy traffic this is comparable to any other major city in the world albeit less expansive. This must have been horrific as your first experience of driving abroad. He told us that at one junction he had taken a turn down a one-way street and was stopped by the Guardia. The Guardia are the military police force and have more authority than your normal police officers in Spain. They carry a gun and as my brother found out it doesn't take much for them to draw it from their holsters.

He was stopped and told to do a three-point turn and to make his way back down the street in the correct direction. He pointed to the end of the street and pleaded to the officers, 'if you just let me go to the end of this street and turn left, I think i know my way home from there.' The Guardia weren't interested, and he was told to turn around immediately. I think the heat and a bit of frustration may have got the better of my brother and he tried to put his point of view across once more. Knowing my brother and his sarcastic sense of humour, his own point of view would have been put quite strongly.

One of the officers decided to show him their point of view and pulled out his gun and pointed it to the air, 'turn around Senor and go the way we say?' My brother could not believe they'd pull a gun on him for a road traffic incident. He did as he was told and probably made the most pressurised three-to-ten-point turn in the whole of Spain that day.

Lanzarote is a place that has the Marmite factor attached to it, some people love it, and some people hate it. I for one think it's a wonderful place with an amazing character that can only be appreciated by those who make the effort to explore the island fully. As a keen bike rider, I've taken the opportunity to visit lots of towns and villages from the northern tip right down to the lava fields of the southwest. It has a terrain like no other place on Earth and was used by NASA for moon buggy tests back in the seventies. It has a live volcano and breath-taking views from various vantage points all over the island. It has kept its heritage and it's unique freshness by not allowing any of its buildings to climb over three storeys high. Cesar Manrique was a famous artist that lived on the island and his artistic signatures can be seen in many places scattered across the landscape. He was hugely popular, and his legacy remains rooted firmly in the Canarian culture to this day. His combination of artistic expression and the importance of keeping the environmental values in place has paid massive dividends. The only building that escaped Cesar Manrique's watchful eye was the seventeen storey Gran Hotel, built in Arrecife. This was constructed in 1988 while the artist was taking some time away from the island. It caused that much controversy that it was left unoccupied for many years, until the local government agreed for it to be redeveloped in 2004.

As with many European destinations including the Canary Islands, the acceptance of tourists and the clash of some cultures will inevitably cause a little friction here and there.

Since travel became more affordable the treaty of Versailles was never more important especially where the Germans are concerned. However, as Michael Neiberg pointed out in his book 'The Concise History,' it is an uneasy peace. Rule one of the treaties mentioned, 'diplomacy.' This was slightly forgotten by our German neighbours during our stay during Christmas 2013. Our friends had decided to join us for a Christmas getaway at an apartment in Puerto del Carmen. We've travelled together on many occasions to lots of destinations and they too have found themselves involved in many of our calamitous situations. The hotel Labranda was a clean and comfortable place to spend a Christmas vacation. The weather was in the high seventies, and we spent plenty of time cooling off in the local bars and in some great tapas restaurants. The second-floor apartment we had been given was spacious and had a good-sized balcony. Below our two second floor apartments were a family that consisted of a couple in their mid-seventies and another couple in their mid-thirties. As we dragged our suitcases to the stairs that ran directly between their room and ours, I made a point of saying good evening. They looked at me like I'd just told them all to go and burn in hell. Puzzled by this, a couple minutes later I walked past them again and this time said 'guten Morgan,' obviously the wrong time of day but at least I was trying to make the effort. Still, they grimaced and looked like they were auditioning for the Adams Family. I thought I may have gotten their nationality wrong, and they may be French or even worse from St Helens. We unpacked our suitcases and got together for a drink on the balcony. While taking in the views of the hotel surroundings, I overheard the family below having a conversation.

To me it all sounded like 'ya, ya, shnoodle doodle and apple strudel ya.' One hundred percent German, i told my wife and friends. We were absolutely amazed when, within the hour a security team person came to our apartments and told us to be a little quieter. Maybe we had been loud, but it wasn't due drink or music, it was merely the sound of unpacking. We became conscious of not letting any chairs scrape along the tiled floor or letting any doors slam shut. We're the type of people who have a lot of respect for other people's peace and quiet and would not deliberately cause any upset. The following day we had another visit from the security team, who this time came as a pair. 'You really must be quieter,' they pleaded in broken English. 'The people below are complaining that you have been noisy all day.' Rule one of the Geneva convention, diplomacy, went straight out the window. Me and my friend asked the security guys to follow us downstairs and so began the inquest. The old German guy spoke good English and as soon as he clasped eyes on us, he knew we weren't there for schnitzel or Schnapps. 'Ya ya you are ruining our holiday, we want to move from here, you English are so bad, noise all of the day.' His wife and his children stood behind him scowling in union. It was then we explained that we had left the apartments early that morning and been out all day at the Lanzarote golf club. We had only just got back to the apartment minutes before the security guys had knocked. We were now staring at four very embarrassed faces. They stopped speaking and I felt like I'd just shot down the Red Barron. But then my dear friend who was fuming at the audacity of these blatant lies suddenly burst out with, 'just because you lost the war, you just can't get over it can you?' Although we had every right to be angry with these worthless accusations, I felt slightly embarrassed at my friends' burning remarks. Resembling the scene from faulty towers I turned to him quickly and said, 'don't mention the war.' My mate Andy had just sent diplomacy packing and to be fair i was also getting sick of trying to prove our innocence. The security guys who i think had no idea of what we were referring to interjected and asked us to go with them to the reception area to calm down, which we did. As we were escorted by security to the reception, I suddenly had a realisation. We passed a large gathering of cleaners who were all huddled together on the path outside of our apartments. They were smoking and chatting loudly, and it was obvious that we and the Germans had been given the worst rooms on the complex.

We overlooked the kitchens and the cleaners' storerooms where they congregated several times a day for a chat and a smoke. This was right in front of the Germans ground floor apartment, and they must have felt like they were in a goldfish bowl. They must have been plotting feverishly to get a move and we were to be their perfect excuse, or so they thought. I asked about them at reception and I was proven correct, they had indeed been asking for a move from the day they'd arrived. The reception also understood our predicament but as the hotel was full, we'd be staying right where we were. We never heard a peep out of our neighbours from that moment on and we made sure our towels were first on the sun beds every morning. They may have bombed our chippies, but they were the ones who got battered, well verbally anyway.

CHAPTER 5

Bullet Proof Brits

Colombia is regarded as the world's most likely place to be kidnapped. Until recently Colombia had the long maintained this dubious title of the kidnapping capital of the world, with 29,000 people being held to ransom, over the past 40 years. But apart from the small risk of getting on the wrong side of the cartel, or being duped into being a drug mule, it's a wonderful place to visit. Maybe Colombia gets a raw deal due to its long-standing relationship with the export of cocaine? However, when entering the port of Cartagena on a cruise ship under a blue sky you get a much better image. It has a skyline of modern high-rise buildings that glimmer under an azure blanket of natural warmth. Cruise ships renowned for their wealth of entertainment along with a promise of an expanding waistline, are a terrific way to arrive in another country. They are the perfect way to visit a multitude of destinations within a limited amount of time and there is a stark difference between arriving by sea than by air. The industry is not just about providing a world of onboard luxury it also combines it with a once in a lifetime experience. As we slowly coasted into Cartagena the wind dropped and the first thing you notice is the dry heat. Dressed in the customary 'look at me I'm a tourist,' outfits we shuffled down the gang plank and took to the colourful bustling streets. After getting through passport control you are quickly bombarded by the local inhabitants who are waving laminated sheets of amazing places to visit. The dockside numbers quickly swell to around two-thousand day trippers who stare apprehensively at the offers of a mystery tour. At the time you can't help but wonder if the unofficial tour ends up with you on a piece of wasteland with empty pockets and a hole in the back of your head. The alternative and perhaps the wiser choice is to go with the registered extortionists, better known as the cruise directors, organised trips. They will sell you the same trip that a local will but for quadruple the price, whose the criminal now. Their main selling pitch is to constantly remind you that the ship won't sail without you if your late getting back. The wife and I did the sensible thing and climbed into a ramshackle minibus with a few other keen savers and headed off to a monastery on the top of a remote hill. The promise of the best views in Cartagena for an extremely competitive price was all it took to win us over. The Monasterio de la Popa was situated high up on what was the only stretch of green landscape for miles around. The journey up the steep hill side was another reminder of the abject poverty that is normally hidden from view and shamefully labelled as someone else's problem. You almost wish you had been blindfolded, due to the amounts of rubbish and squaller that weaves between the corrugated shacks like a giant anaconda. Considered as home to so many of the inhabitants who sit statuesque staring into an invisible void. The air conditioning in the van is nothing more than a small plastic fan plugged in to the cigarette lighter on the dashboard. You really can't complain as you gulp down the warm Evian water that is far cleaner than anything the locals get from a tap. The road to the monastery was a combination of rubble and deep potholes. Every so often we'd be thrown from our seats and a cheery apology would be called out by the driver. We were surrounded by thick lush vegetation which looked to be a cross between a jungle and a typical English forest back home. There were palm trees spaced sporadically alongside the edges of the road next to overgrown bushes and vines that crept their way through broken fences and old abandoned cars. Clusters of tall trees stretched defiantly to the sky between fragile houses acting like mother nature's army protecting her poorest children below.

Our dusty white bus rattled its way into a small car park perched at the top of the hill and it we felt slightly relieved to have made it thus far. Stepping off the bus hardly made any difference to the temperatures we'd already endured; we were now acclimatised from being cooped up in the mobile greenhouse. The clearing allowed the afternoon sun to drench this remote open space with oppressive humidity, so although we were effectively higher, it wasn't any cooler. It felt fitting to be visiting a place of worship on a Christmas Eve and although there wasn't going to be any snow the spirit of Christmas was more than evident. Religion is not one of my strongest points and yet I was more than humbled by the gestures that were taking place. Outside the monastery local children had gathered to receive gifts from the resident monks. Footballs and dollies were being handed out to lots of happy smiling faces who looked like they had indeed inherited the earth. The small car park started to fill with other tourists who had also bought into this journey of enlightenment. It soon became a thriving hub of photo hungry visitors and local entrepreneurs selling everything from hats to recycled water, which also came in an Evian bottle. There were a few older men carrying sloths across their arms and over their shoulders, offering tourists a chance to have their photograph taken with this native sleepy creature. A large grey donkey stood patiently with its ears protruding through a sombrero, just like the ones you see on an old Blackpool postcard. It was decorated in a multi coloured woollen blanket which in my eyes was akin to cruelty. It had probably been ridden to the top of the hill by its podgy owner, only to be rewarded by having an overweight tourist plonked on its back. Our minibus driver who also doubled as tour guide was standing alongside something that looked like a toll booth. It had an old turnstile attached to it, that allowed entrance into the monastery which was built in 1607. The turnstile looked like it had been taken from an old football ground. Although we were the first group of tourists to arrive, we found ourselves being the last in line behind a small but moving queue. We stood patiently waiting for the driver to finish his negotiations to get us through at no extra cost. Strange how you must pay to get into a place of worship, when you can pray anywhere, even on a plane.

I'm not aware of how much the driver had to pay to get us in to this holy establishment but I imagine it was-far less than the money we'd paid to get into head office back in Rome. Then, from out of nowhere, the unmistakable sound of a gunshot. It was quickly followed by the sound of another bullet being fired, which built into a crescendo of rapid machine gun fire. All around us mass panic broke out with bare footed children running into the forest screaming and shouting in fear. The donkey broke loose from its owner braying loudly like a petrified Zebra being chased by a lion. Somehow it recognised the change of atmosphere and decided to raise the alarm by braying loudly and pulling at its reigns. Breaking free, It set off into a gallop and headed off back down the hill, with its owner chasing frantically behind. There was no pinning the tail on this donkey, the party was over, and freedom beckoned.

The sloth which is one of the slowest creatures on Earth was now hurtling down the hill at a tremendous speed wrapping its long arms around its owners neck and holding on for dear life. Our party stood motionless queueing in an orderly fashion waiting to be beckoned past the turnstile. The machine gun fire continued in short bursts. 'Is that real gun fire?' someone asked. We all stared at each other nervously. 'Sounds like it,' said another voice from the queue. 'Get down, get down,' came the drivers startled voice from the front of the queue beneath the shelter of the wooden turnstile. A gate swung open adjacent to the payment kiosk, and we were asked to keep our heads down and step through quickly. Like a human caterpillar we crawled our way through to safety still under fire. Once in the confinement of the monastery walls one of our group asked the driver if it was genuine bullet fire we'd heard? He gave an apologetic smile and nodded his head. 'There is a military base in the woods hidden just behind the monastery and sometimes local people will climb the fence to steal from the soldiers' barracks. They are after their boots because they are very valuable here. The soldiers fire their guns into the trees to frighten them off and if someone gets hurt or killed, they will say that they should not have been there.' His answer came as so matter of fact that it only added to the hypocrisy of our surroundings. The monastery was decorated in rich bright colours with religious artefacts hanging from every wall. Woven tapestry's depicting famous biblical stories covered the polished wooden floors and hung-over heavy wooden bannisters. Large white candles burned tirelessly in small alcoves, highlighting the tall golden candelabras that held them in place. The guide took immense pleasure in bringing the paintings and sculptures to life by revealing the history behind each portrait. At the centre of the monastery there was an open courtyard that featured baskets of flowers and small palms which added even more colour beyond the paintings. Beyond the courtyard and through some heavy iron doors there was a pathway that led outside onto a veranda . From here we could see the city of Cartagena going about its business one hundred and fifty metres below our feet. Above us, Turkey vultures circled effortlessly on the thermal uplifts, waiting to spot a free lunch, thankfully it wasn't on the car park. 'And now we go to the city,' announced the driver pointing the way back to the minibus. We filed back through the turnstile and out onto the car park were we were greeted by yet more children and more traders. Business had quickly resumed, and additional tourists were still arriving by the coach load. After declining a photograph with a venomous looking yellow snake which was to be hung around my neck, we finally climbed back onboard our bus. As we rumbled our way back down the hill towards the old city centre, we passed the old man and his donkey working their back way back up the steep hill. He was digging his heels into his trusty servant, encouraging it to put some extra effort into its stride. He knew that profits were down, and every minute counted so he rode that poor donkey like it was the favourite in the Grand National. Incidentally neither him nor the donkey had shoes.

Cartagena is a combination of the old and new worlds. It's city streets have beautiful old cafes and genteel bars where they serve the Colombian national drink 'Aguardiente,' or firewater as it's known. Around every corner there seems to be historical local markets selling the same garbage to tourists here as they do in Europe. There is no escaping the yapping mechanical dog or someone firing a flashing whirly thing into the air. The Hard Rock Café staff were busy pulling in any passers-by who had earlier stood beneath the statue of Admiral Blas De LeZo wondering who is this guy? The plaque is written in Spanish and if you could read it, you would discover that he was South Americas equivalent of Admiral Lord Nelson. One eye, one arm and one leg, this tough old sea dog kicked the British navy's backside in 1741 during the battle of Cartagena. Admiral De Lezo had his leg amputated during this famous battle after being hit by a cannon ball. Out gunned and outnumbered he'd kicked the arse of the British fleet who were ordered to retreat to Jamaica to lick their wounds. Having spent a wonderful day drinking Land Shark beer in Montego Bay, it certainly makes sense for a great retreat. Although my visit to Jamaica was a brief stopover which consisted of beach, snorkelling and beer, it would be fair to say that I probably left the island in the same state as the Admiral, legless.

CHAPTER 6

Ask the Captain

There is nothing more exciting than your first cruise holiday and what could be better than staying in and sailing out of New York for the first time? The city that never sleeps is even more awake at Christmas. We landed at JFK the day before New Year's Eve and made our way into Manhattan by means of a luxury coach provided by the tour company. Staring out of the window the city slowly creeps up on you. It quickly gets busier, taller, and more populated as you journey into the district of Queens. To get across the river you traverse across the Queensboro bridge and suddenly the concrete and steel begin to dominate the skyline. In truth the sky almost disappears from sight, hidden by the huge buildings that lean right over you. This must be what an ant feels like when climbing a wall. You get the impression that you've been dropped into a blockbuster movie set and that you are somewhere between reality and Gotham city. It was 2002 when we first visited New York, the year after the attack on the twin towers and the level of security was still visibly high. We stared out of the window as at huge cavalcade of police cars that drove in procession past our coach with sirens blaring and blue lights flashing. Was this normal we asked each other? Maybe they're making a movie or still on high alert after 911, we tried to think of all the possible reasons. It only takes a few seconds before your attention is diverted to yet another eye-catching statement of human activity. This is the big Apple, allegedly named after a horse track reference and nothing to do with the fruit itself. The city skyscrapers inflict constant neck pain as they induce you to make vertical glances to their distant peaks. Every building seems to shimmer as thousands of windows reflect light back onto the streets with no names. This is indeed the human equivalent of an ant's nest with people scurrying in every direction. It's alive with ingenuity and purpose and their home is built on twenty-two square miles of effective collaboration. With no space to expand it grows vertically creating living spaces as high as 541 metres.

As part of our 'stay and cruise,' we had been given a room at the Crown Plaza hotel on 42nd street which was in mid down Manhattan. It was a terrific location situated on the doorstep of some iconic buildings. The Empire State Building and the Chrysler building were a five-minute walk away and Grand Central station was also just around the corner, or as they say in New York 'a block away.' New York is a demanding city, and you need lots of energy to get the best out of it. Grand central station became one of our favourite locations due to it's amazing architecture which in some ways felt too good to be a train station. It's timeless and breath-taking with its sleek beaux arts design and its famous opal faced clock as its centre piece. Not including passengers, it has over twenty-eight million visitors a year making it one of the top ten visitor attractions in the world. We decided to take the train to see ground zero as it had been converted into a site for people to pay their respects. We were sure that the ticket booth agent had told us platform four, but it soon became apparent that we had jumped on the wrong train and were heading in the wrong direction. The carriage was standing room only, due to it being the rush hour. It had begun its journey from somewhere in the business district of lower Manhattan. An announcement came over the carriage PA explaining that this was a direct none stop train for Harlem, and it would be making only one stop at some station we'd never heard of. The train in proportion was predominantly filled with black and mixed-race people except for the two confused white people who were the only two people carrying a New York subway train map. What's more and even cringingly stereotypical of a couple of white people, the word Harlem had induced an irrational fear due to all the seventies series we'd watched as kids. When I was a kid, Kojak was called to solve a murder in either Brooklyn or Harlem every week. There were only two places in New York when i was a teenager growing up in the seventies. Nobody got murdered in Greenwich village or the upper east side, they just argued over works of art and which restaurants to visit. In my mind we were on the express train to murdersville. We whispered in agreement that the next stop was ours, were ever it was. The plan we quickly surmised, was that there must be a train heading back in the opposite direction and we were going to get straight back on it. The train gave an angry high-pitched squeal as it pulled into the darkest underground train station on planet Earth. We were the only two people to step off the train and no one else had joined us. As the train set off towards another rat hole of human ingenuity, we stared despairingly at the poorly lit platform straight out of a horror movie. If the station name had been called Elm Street, it would have made perfect sense. We clung to each other so tightly that any passer-by would have mistaken us for Siamese twins. We found a flight of stairs that had a sign on the wall with an arrow pointing down, with the words, 'west bound - track 2.' We now had no choice but to set off to an even deeper place in the bowels of the hell. A couple of strangers passed us on the stairs and at no point did we exchange glances or attempt to give a fake smile. We hot footed it through a network of tunnels with dirty brick walls and exposed cast iron pipes that constantly dripped some kind of liquid onto the resin flooring. We felt like fish out of water waiting to be sliced, diced and gutted, as we swerved the stagnant pools and made our way through a long corridor. We ascended another long flight of stairs which brought us out onto a long well-lit platform which was full of people heading in our direction. We were relieved to hear an announcement telling us the next train was heading to Lower Manhattan. Almost an hour after we had left Grand Central Station, we finally found ourselves in Fulton Street, staring at a bleak empty space. An empty space in Manhattan was usually a small park, everything else has a building on it. A small walkway with a long queue of people took us up to a temporary building that housed a very moving and haunting memorial to those who had lost their lives during the terrifying attack on the 11th of September. The walkway had been set up with huge black and white images, showing people who had perished or worked tirelessly during the disaster. Haunting photographs of twisted beams of metal reminding people of all that remained after the dust and smoke had settled. Looking out onto what was now a building site in a state of rapid development, you couldn't help but notice the void. When it comes to building and development, hardly any ground remains untouched in Manhattan and every square foot has some form of construction sitting on its valuable land. This giant gaping hole was like the space left after you've had a tooth extraction. It was ugly yet tender. It felt empty and painful, and the healing process was going to take time. The blood that once belonged to the innocent and the brave had long since evaporated into the heavens. The dark December sky smothered the city in a veil of ugly grey clouds, releasing countless tears of empathy on the remnants below. The madness that had engulfed this metropolis bringing the entire world to a standstill was now etched into the history books as 911. From here we set off on foot and as per usual, ended up lost in what was now a deserted Wall Street. Considering we were in one of the most crowded cities on the planet we suddenly found ourselves alone again and feeling vulnerable. Thankfully we managed to hail a passing yellow cab which took us back to our hotel. We woke up early the next morning to an unusually warm New Year's Eve and after breakfast set off again, determined to take in as much of the city as we could. The newspapers were full of pictures of Saddam Hussein's death by hanging, administered by the newly formed Iraqi government. We had packed for what was supposed to be a renowned bitter wind chill. The front page of the newspapers weren't just reserved for the death of Saddam Hussein, they were also full of the bizarre twist in weather patterns. The snow in California and the warm blue skies currently in New York were causing quite a stir and had never been witnessed at this time of the year. Lessons in social etiquette came thick and fast in Manhattan and my first encounter was in a bar across the street from our hotel. I was initially taken in by the décor of the McFadden bar and restaurant that resembled the famous Boston Cheers bar, as seen on TV. I climbed onto a bar stool and ordered a pint of Guinness and was attentively served by a bar tender wearing a white apron. He even put a coaster under my glass. I was already taken by the ambience and decided it would be a good idea to try a different beer by the name of Samuel Adams. Try as i might. I couldn't get the bar tender's attention. He blatantly ignored me and served those around me without a second glance. It was then I noticed that each bar fly like myself was putting a dollar down next to their drink as a tip. I hadn't done this earlier and therefore I found myself being permanently snubbed. The culture of tipping in New York stretches down to every type of service you can imagine. I wouldn't be surprised that if you asked someone the time in Manhattan, they would expect a tip. The lessons continued and the biggest lesson of all was when I visited a breakfast deli on the corner of our street. I stood alongside nine or ten busy locals who were making their way to work with no time to spare. We lined up facing a glass counter which had a huge menu board stretching right along the back wall. When I was asked for my order, I duly began to read out the items on the board behind the busy cooks and order takers. 'I'll have two eggs on a cheese bagel please with extra bacon. Can I also have the pancakes and two coffees one black one white.' The angry Impatient six-foot six giant who was already stood on an elevated parapet behind the glass counter stared viciously at me. 'For Christ's sake buddy just give me the dam numbers on the board, Sheeezus?' Nervously I stared past him and stuttered my way through, 'two twos, two eights,' and before I could finish, he asked if I wanted 'cwaffee?' 'Yes, please one black one white.' The queue naturally side stepped one pace towards the end of the counter where a woman on a cash register took your money no questions asked her lips never moved. I was part of a line dance that included service without a smile, but still had a tip jar at the till. I headed back to the hotel carrying hot brown paper bags feeling like I'd been threatened by the school bully on my first day. The following day and much the wiser I stood in the same queue ready to rattle off my numbers like Carol Vorderman on Countdown. 'A two, a six, two fours and two coffees one black, one white to go.' It felt like I was heading for a 'gee buddy now you're talking.' But it wasn't to be, what I did get which I wasn't expecting was, 'you want the eggs, over easy?' Oh my god, that was like being asked to spell diarrhoea. 'Yeh sure,' I replied, with no idea of what my easy eggs would look like. Alongside me in the queue I heard a more familiar voice. It was the unmistakable accent of someone from the U.K. Wigan or Bolton was my closest guess, either way an undeniably strong northern accent. 'Two bacon barms reet and av ya got a sausage barm, two tha knows.' The guy taking the order just stared at him blankly. He didn't even speak or advise like the way he'd kindly advised me the day before, he just continued to stare with bewilderment. I guess in New York he'd come across every type of broken English from every corner of the world. But nowt like this he hadn't. I couldn't stand the silence any longer, they were like two gunslingers before a shoot-out. I quickly intervened and told the Lancashire cowboy to call out the numbers on the board and be quick. The three of us exchanged glances, eyes darting side to side, it was the reminiscent of the ending to, 'The Good the Bad and the Ugly.' Just like the western the tension was unbearable. Then the guy from Wigan drew first, 'all reet then I'll have one of them tha twos, one of them tha ones reet and a foor.' Yes, foor, or fuer, God knows how they pronounce it, but they believe it's a four. If the bad guy behind the counter had a gun, he would have most definitely drawn first and shot him there and then. I don't believe the ugly guy from Wigan left with anything close to what he thought he'd ordered but I felt good that the swearing and shouting from behind the counter wasn't aimed at me. The pace of Manhattan is relentless, only tourists and tortoises move slower. You can spot a sightseer by the way they cross the road. Clutching a map and staring towards the top of a skyscraper, they are oblivious to the oncoming traffic. Mesmerised by the Art Deco at the top of the Chrysler building, it could well be the last thing they ever see on earth before being hit by a yellow cab. In a short three days we took in as many of the famous landmarks as was humanly possible, from the top of the Empire State Building to Times Square. We were advised by some locals not to go to Times Square for New Year's Eve as they said it was not a great experience and easy to lose each other. We opted for a restaurant instead which turned out to be an excellent choice. After a tasty meal in the aptly named Hudson Bay, we crossed the street and brought in the new year in an Irish bar. New Year's Day we were up early in the morning, and we gathered in the hotel lobby with a small crowd of people who were also sailing to the Caribbean aboard the Norwegian Spirit. We were picked up by a coach and taken to the opposite side of Manhattan along forty second street to pier twelve where our ship was docked. She had arrived late in to New York, which meant that all her next passengers were being placed into a holding area that was crammed, humid and uncomfortable. The conditions stifled the excitement, and we felt an air of impatience as all passengers went through a registration process that was long and tiresome. When our names were eventually called out to board the Norwegian Spirit our excitement was instantly reignited. Your first steps onto a cruise ship are never equalled, especially on one that sails out of New York in the dark. The Manhattan skyline looked like the massive spaceship in Spielberg's Close Encounters as we drifted past the iconic Statue of Liberty. To the tunes of a Caribbean steel band, we passed under the Verrazano bridge with the music intensifying the atmosphere to another level. The clear night sky drew in a chilly sea breeze that swirled around the deck as the ship pushed further into the Atlantic. The rest of the evening was spent exploring the decks and of course some fine dining. Part of the way into this cruise we were

quite surprised when we were chosen to be the captains dining companions. Seen by many as a privilege we thought of it as more of a nice invitation. We had received a phone call from reception telling us we'd been chosen to dine with the crew and initially i replied 'we'll give it a miss.' But the receptionist nearly died and said, 'please don't decline as you have been chosen to dine with the captain tomorrow.' We didn't want to let the main man down, so we accepted although god knows why he chose us. When the evening came, we took our seats with the two other guests. One guest was a Welsh lady who had previously produced television programmes for the BBC and the other was an elderly gentleman from Norway. The captain also being from Norway later explained, that the elderly guy was a naval war hero. I noticed he had no fingers on his left hand which was something to do with him escaping a sinking battleship and miraculously getting to Jamaica. Seems to be a popular place to go if you're getting your arse kicked in war times. What is it with heroic sailors having to be minus body parts? The captain was a good host and we asked him a variety of questions about his life away from the ship. We talked about everything from football to questions about his family. He told us how he enjoys going fishing with his sons back in Norway and how beautiful his country was. It seemed all eyes were upon us from the other tables of which there were many. The other guests, mostly American sat with other members of the crew. I could feel an air of resentment and subconsciously thought that the other diners where wondering 'why them?' Yet id have been just as happy to sit with someone from the engineering department. Later that evening when we finally got back to our cabin, we found a letter that had been pushed under the door. It read, *'you have been chosen to dine with the captain and you will be his guests for the evening. Please keep your conversation based to questions regarding the ship and its crew. Please feel free to ask the captain any questions regarding the history and the running of the Norwegian Spirit. Have a wonderful evening.'*
In truth we had not asked him a single question about the ship

and I'm sure he was grateful for it. By the next morning we were sailing off the coast of Florida with the warm wind disguising the true temperature. I found this out after slapping a bottle of oil all over me and burning to a deep crimson red. I looked like a hog roast and suffered for days which was nothing unusual for me.

One of the big attractions on most cruise ships is the onboard casino which truly fascinated me. Here you get to see the high rollers with money to spare and they all seem to have a brash and carefree attitude. For me it was a chance to watch the range of emotions that people display when they are at their most vulnerable. I never really got to grips with the rules that governed these games and the craps table and blackjack were lost on me entirely. But I slowly worked out the roulette table odds and decided to give it a go. Lesson one, you can't hand the croupier your money it has to be placed on the table, this is so the overhead cameras can see the transaction. If there's a dispute regarding any movement of chips or money, the cameras get called into action. The discreet cameras and their operators probably keep a keen eye out for any staff pocketing money or punters cheating. I placed my twenty dollars in front of the croupier, and he gave me twenty-one-dollar chips. I picked a few numbers and put a couple on red. My heart was in my mouth as the white ball bounced and rattled its way on to a red number and I joined in with my compatriots who gave out a winning cheer. My two dollars was now four, but I'd lost four dollars on single numbers. I put a few chips on groups of numbers but they and my beginner's luck soon dwindled away. I then realised that while I was putting a dollar chip on a single number, other people were throwing around multiple bets using twenty-five-dollar chips, stacking one on top of another. I was embarrassed but you'd never have noticed, I was already as red as half of the numbers on the wheel. While I was losing my pocket money, my wife was winning two hundred dollars on a slot machine that she had no idea how to play. The trick here is to remember it's a playground for the wealthy. It's easy to get carried away and one must be prepared to leave with empty pockets.   After several cruises you begin to see through the glitz and glamour and you learn that the Dickie bow brigade are the remnants of another era, somewhere between the Titanic and a funeral parlour. An evening gown doesn't mean your wealthy and the un-happy waiter can still spit in your dinner. While sailing on a P and O cruise out of Barbados I met the comedian Roy Walker, relaxing after finishing a performance of his one man show. He was sitting alone with a glass of wine and smoking a large cigar. It was late and I was sitting with a beer and a cigarette at a table opposite.   I'm not sure how, but we slowly struck up conversation. He wasn't fond of the ship or the crew for that matter and he gave the impression of being bored with the whole cruise in its entirety. I was careful not to get into anything involving his career as I often feel that celebrities like the captain of a ship must get asked the same questions repeatedly. His earlier show was based on anecdotes about the famous comedians he'd worked with. Bernard Manning, George Roper, Charlie Williams and Ken Goodwin all of whom featured in his humorous recollections.   Of course, for anyone who is not familiar with those well-known names from the seventies it would have been a long show indeed. Roy was subdued and i felt he would rather be anywhere than on the Azura in the Caribbean. I'm not the type of person who would start gushing when meeting a celebrity as very often they are either narcissistic or as dull as dishwater. It's nice to appreciate their art or skill and be respectful but the last thing they want is some fanatic asking them what's their favourite colour is. I once stood outside Manchester airport wearing smart golfing attire, holding two bags of clubs along with professional looking travel bags and waited patiently while my friend went to park the car. We were heading to Spain and the early morning seemed to be unusually quiet and devoid of other travellers. A smart black car similar to a limousine pulled up near to where I was standing and out got Ruud Van Nistelrooy the prolific Manchester United striker. Manchester United were playing in the FA cup final at the Cardiff Millennium stadium due to the new Wembley stadium getting built. He was sporting a black blazer with the club's badge emblazoned on the chest pocket. He took his bag from the driver and walked in my direction staring at me intently. The entrance to the terminal was behind me and as he headed for the doors, he gave me a puzzled, '*do I know you,*' sort of stare. He smiled raised his hand and quietly said 'hi.' I did nothing except say 'hi,' back. Minutes later another black limo pulled up and Christiano Ronaldo steps out, dressed in the same black blazer. He also took his bag from the driver, which is ironic because some time later I took a driver from my bag! He too followed the same path and actions as Rudd Van Nistelrooy, waving with a toothy white smile and staring at me with the 'should I know him expression?' He looked back at me again as he walked through the airport entrance doors. Either they are both extremely polite, or they thought I was a fellow pro, and they couldn't take the chance that I may end up sitting next to them on a Question of Sport. I told my mate when he got back and being a fellow Evertonian he was unimpressed. I can't remember exactly what he said but something along the lines of 'pair of tossers.' Those pair of tossers both went on to score in the 2004 final against Millwall winning three nil, Nistelrooy got two Ronaldo one. I wonder if they asked each other on the plane, 'do you know who that tosser was with the golf bag?'

Back on the Norwegian Spirit, life was just one long food fest. Walking may be good exercise, but you could easily put on a stone walking from one end of the ship to another. I'm no athlete but you will see some of the biggest people pigging out on a cruise. Multitudes of obese people can be seen sweating profusely while gorging on the sumptuous food and buckets of beer. Attending the breakfast buffet is like a bun fight and you can often find yourself hemmed in by a clone of Pavarotti on your left and Andre the giant on your right. Over the ten years we spent traveling on cruises we witnessed the changes as the market started to attract and cater for a younger audience. Cruises became more fashionable with better onboard facilities and newer attractions. The ships suddenly got bigger and the misconception that cruises were just for the rich, old and wrinkly was being swept away. With Ice rinks and climbing walls, water slides and night clubs, the cruise lines were changing their demographics quickly. The younger audience with money to burn were being offered something that normally appealed to those who had retired with a healthy pension. By the time we'd reached our seventh cruise the mobility scooter brigade had arrived, and the elderly were taking back their territory. Like a tank division they blocked off as many strategic areas of the ship as they could. They were cleverly camouflaged, and you couldn't see the scooter beneath the twenty-five stones that glided effortlessly past the cocktail bar. A flowing multi coloured sequined evening dress was used to cleverly hide their four wheeled chariot below. These cruiser weights often came in twos, with the male normally wearing an audacious Hawaiian shirt and beige tight-fitting shorts. Very often it is only the bushier overgrown walrus moustache and evening dress that helps to tell them apart. Not content with taking a leisurely drive around the deck they flick the switch from tortoise mode to rabbit mode and hurtle around the atrium like Lewis Hamilton fighting for pole position. A quick pit stop at 'Carlos Steak House, 'for refuelling and then on to the theatre to see some paper thin human beings performing 'Cats,' While us fatties are getting fatter the skinnies are getting thinner. After working out in the gym all day they have worked up a well-deserved appetite. That's when you see the stick insect in front of you at the buffet picking up a lettuce leaf, a bowl of soup and a crouton. How do they do it?

For thousands of years the oceans have called out to many nations to venture across its great vastness. From Viking long boats to Spanish galleons, the most daring discoveries were made in vessels that leaked and creaked against the fiercest of conditions. History tells us that life on the cruel sea was the hardest life of all. Even with today's more modern vessels the possibility of been snared by a raging storm is something still to be respected. Today's trawler men are listed as having the second most dangerous job on the planet the first is apparently an oil rig diver. Thankfully there is more chance of dying from choking on a meatball than being killed by a cannon ball on the ocean these days. This apart from falling overboard, makes the restaurant the most dangerous place on the ship. As if to prove a point while sailing on the Celebrity Millennium, my wife and I had booked a unique dining experience. We had managed to reserve a table at the exclusive Olympic restaurant. This lavishly decorated room had some of the original panelling from the RMS Olympics', al la Carte restaurant. Acquired from the original ship built in 1911 she was known for being the sister ship of the Titanic. On our arrival the Maître d linked my wife's arm and showed us to our table, all very posh indeed. I couldn't help but feel the nostalgia wash over me and i decided that I'd allow myself to wallow in this simulated piece of history.

I was transported easily to another era and if the night ended up with me clinging to a raft in some freezing cold water I would not have been surprised. Thankfully, the only ice floating in water on this particular evening was inside the glass jug on our table. The sommelier introduced himself with his taste-vine hanging around his neck, which if I'm honest I had no idea what it was. The taste-vine or the 'Tastevin' as it is officially known is more for show than for its original purpose. Basically, it's a bottle opener and a saucer to test the wine from. I'm sure if there's a sommelier reading this, they would probably choke on their Romanée-Conti. We were offered distinct types of wines that would complement the five or so courses we had chosen and refused them all. We asked for a bottle of Berringer and a beer which brought about an expression of disgust from our learned friend. He looked like he was sucking on a lemon and pursed his lips and cheeks similar to the look Kenneth Williams used to give in the Carry-On films. Without a word he set off to another table to find some real fine diners. The starters arrived in a small silver cloche, i had chosen a mushroom soup with a foam. It tasted bloody awful, and i can only describe it as drinking muddy water.   Why or how I can compare it with soil I can't be too sure, but that's how it came across, maybe chef had left a clod of mud on one of the mushrooms or on one of his wellies? I supposed that by now the waiters had worked out that we were from below decks and would be just as at home eating a meal with someone stoking a boiler or doing the laundry. The restaurant was full and yet there could not have been more than fifteen to twenty tables. As we waited for our second course my wife who is more the observant noticed an incident taking place on the table opposite. A man aged somewhere in his mid-seventies was dining with his wife along with his son and his girlfriend. His son who would have been in his late thirties had left the table to go to the bathroom as the Americans call it. My wife had nudged me with her elbow to get me to look at the elderly gentleman's face which was quickly turning into a dark shade of purple. Like a felled tree his face slammed into his plate of food with a loud crash. His wife called out his name several times while also crying out for help. No one moved a muscle, the waiters stood as if their shiny brogues had been nailed to the floor. The Maître D took out his mobile from his pocket and looked like he was calling a friend in a calm and casual manner. 'Help them Lester,' pleaded my wife having assessed the situation and realising that the room had turned in to a portrait of Da Vinci's 'Last Supper,' nobody was moving. I felt tentative and had a *'why me,'* moment but made my way over to their table with some urgency. My first thought was that his airway maybe blocked, and he was choking. The fact that he was no longer conscious made me doubt that he was choking as you would normally associate this with some noise and a fighting for breath, it had gone far beyond that. The situation became worse, because I suddenly became aware that this man was in a wheelchair. He looked like he'd done plenty of fine dining too, his portly frame was wedged firmly into the steep sides of his chair.

I looked around the room in the vein hope that I'd be joined by an extra pair of helping hands. No willing volunteers came forward, so It looked odds on that this was going to be this guy's last supper after all. It was unnerving as it felt like I was taking part in some sort of Victorian parlour game. Just as I was lifting the man from his chair his son arrived and he quickly realised the situation. He shouted for his father to respond and pulled him out of his chair by tucking his arms under his fathers' arms. 'Help me take the weight,' he instructed me with the upmost urgency. He was a tall, well-built man and he lifted his father with the intention of performing the Heimlich manoeuvre. This wouldn't be easy with a dead weight, so I kneeled on the floor and took the weight from underneath. We worked to a rhythm, he pulled up on his father's abdomen and I pushed up from below. Each lift from his son came with a loud fart and I was strangely embarrassed that the onlookers may think it was me. It got worse, as beads of sweat quickly gathered on my forehead and i somehow managed to slip my head between this man's legs. Something popped into my head from the numerous first aid training courses that I'd attended and that was to loosen a tie or undo a collar button to help ease air way restrictions. I will never know how I managed to do this, but I reached up with one arm and did exactly that. 'Come on pop, come on pop, 'his son called out, voice trembling in desperation. I knew it was pointless to continue with the Heimlich manoeuvre more than five times and we'd gone well beyond that. My position had become intolerable and extremely uncomfortable, so I called out loudly to lay the man onto the floor. I was physically trapped and was beginning to match the colour of the guy we were trying to help. My head felt like it was clamped in a vice and about to be crushed. The on lookers laughed, yes, they actually laughed at my predicament. I don't think they were laughing at the desperate plight of this young man and his father, but I do think my head sticking out from the crotch of a fat guy and being forced to literally carry his weight was too much to bear for some of the audience. I checked for a pulse and felt for breath on the back of my hand of which there was neither. I was about to perform CPR for the second time in my life when a crash team of medics came dashing into the room and thankfully took over. They stretchered the man out of the restaurant who was followed by his worried and tearful family.

I returned to my seat lathered in sweat and totally dishevelled. I was foaming at the mouth, and it had nothing to do with the crap mushroom soup I'd tackled earlier. I'd no sooner sat down when a waiter appeared at my side and presented me with a steak dinner. 'Are you kidding me, did you not see what's just happened?' I barked at him abruptly. 'Take it away,' I said, still gasping for breath, amazed at his lack of compassion for the situation. After gulping down a large glass of cheap but affordable Beringer I began to regain my composure. The atmosphere was still low key, and I began to dwell on the events wondering if the man had recovered. The only time I'd performed CPR was the day I'd passed my 'first aid course.' I had the certificate in my hand when an old lady keeled over in front of me. It was in a shopping centre and for one fleeting moment I thought it was a set up. By the time an ambulance had arrived both me and another first aider had got her breathing again. The lady was in her nineties and sadly she passed away later that evening in hospital. Her son who worked for the local police force managed to track me down and knocked on my door that night to thank me for my efforts. So, my life saving skills thus far were one nil to the grim reaper. The Olympic restaurant slowly returned to a quietly reserved chatter, which no doubt had the recent events as the focal point of its conversations. Spoons full of caviar washed down with a glass of Dom Pérignon and explanations of how they were just about to help. The old, 'I'd have stabbed him in the throat with a biro,' would have been up there along with an emergency lung draining thoracostomy. About thirty to forty minutes had passed when the son of the man in the wheelchair walked purposefully back into the restaurant and up to our table. 'My dad's fine and he's sitting up, I wanted to come back and say thank you for all of your help.' I probably smiled and said no problem glad to hear he's ok, I don't recall exactly. What I do remember was how he turned to the

91

maître d and the waiters and tongue lashed them for not offering any assistance. The maître d held his mobile aloft trying to point out that it was his call that brought in the crash team. To be fair his actions probably saved the old man's life. But the truth of the matter is rather concerning. How many people have jobs that are involved with public services and have no idea of first aid? You would think that the crew of a cruise ship would have been through an induction that had first aid training high on its agenda.

Another common fact is that cruise ships are very prone to the threat of Norovirus, apparently lurking in every corner waiting to kill off the weak and infirm. My wife and I both took ill with severe chest infections on one cruise, and we ended up not being able to leave the cabin for days. My wife became so poorly, and her breathing became so difficult that we needed to visit the ships doctor. The doctor had a well-equipped surgery including the help of a nursing assistant. They quickly put my wife on a nebuliser and took some blood samples. Within minutes her blood was spinning around in a centrifuge device and being analysed for information. The practice room looked like it belonged to Dr Frankenstein, and I would not have been surprised to see a bit of lightening jumping between two rods. It suddenly dawned on me that this wasn't the good old NHS, it was private treatment on a cruise ship in the middle of the Caribbean. How expensive could this be? I told my wife I'd go and check our on-board credit and see if I could get an idea of what the bill was going to look like and see if we'd be waiting on tables for the rest of the cruise. In the time it took me to get from the lowest deck on the ship to the purser's desk, the bill had already been calculated and fed into the ship's computer. I presented my onboard sea pass, which is basically a credit card created by the ship which I'd loaded with two thousand dollars when first boarding the ship. We hadn't spent any money since we'd both been confined to our sick bed, so apart from the medical bill I expected the balance to be somewhat healthy. I was very much mistaken, for ten minutes work the medical crew had raided our holiday spends. These pirates of the Caribbean had taken one thousand dollars for their services. My wife's blood was spinning below deck while my head was spinning above deck. I took the lift back to the medical room and smiled at my wife as I entered the room. It was one of those Hollywood movie type smiles, where the director would have said, I want you to smile like you're trying to hide something but at the same time look concerned. I did this so well my wife intuitively knew what had happened. 'How much,' she asked, breathing deeply from beneath the clear visor supplying her oxygen. I told her straight with the selfishness of a man who was just about breathing himself. 'Oh my god,' she spluttered taking the mask away from her face as if it would stop some invisible cash counter that was adding dollars to the bill with every breath she took. I told her to put the mask back on as she was now gasping for air but with eyes filled with tears. My wife had been suffering from severe asthma attacks for many years and carried inhalers everywhere she went. Sometimes during severe bouts of gasping for breath she would need steroids to get her back on track. When our beloved cat Oscar died after thirteen years my wife no longer needed an inhaler and never suffered another chest infection again. We put two and two together and spent ages deep cleaning the house making sure that any tiny flake of Oscar was hoovered and polished into oblivion. We would put Oscar in a cattery whenever we went on holiday. The lovely woman who ran this five-star cat hotel asked me if I wanted to ring Oscar while we were away. I don't think she or I could have described my expression at that precise moment. I stared open mouthed at her not moving or blinking for a short time trying to contain my disbelief that someone would possibly think that i would pay to make a call to a cat. What would I say?

'Pssss pssss psssss, Oscaaaar can you hear me?
'Have you made any friends yet?'
'What's the food like?'

'Is the strange woman looking after you alright?'
Silence.......
'Ahh you're angry with us?'
'I understand you're pissed off for being caged for two weeks, not even a meow?'
' Suit yourself, i actually don't care, because including your cattery fee, you just cost me well over a thousand dollars you mingy moggie!'
(of course, i didn't know this was about to happen re medical fees)

Sorry Mrs loony cat woman, but we've had Oscar for twelve years now and he's never uttered a word, so that's a no, we won't be calling Oscar ship to shore, not now, not ever.

I understand that you must be doing this for some other peculiar like-minded people, holding your mobile phone to Fluffy's ear while they tell Fluffy how much they love and miss them. Personally, i think these people probably belong in a similar cage to Fluffy, but with a little more padding.

I'll come back onto cruising later as its so expansive, i can't do it justice in one single chapter.
Did I say expansive? I meant expensive.

CHAPTER 7

What Can Go Wrong?

The airport queue at check in has the ability to make or break a holiday. We usually stay at an airport hotel the night before a flight, benefiting from the relaxation and avoiding any possible car problems. It's great to be able to relax and have the car parked on site, knowing it's going to be ready for the journey home. On one occasion we had checked into a hotel at Manchester airport on Christmas Day and were looking forward to our flight to JFK New York with a connecting flight to Miami. The hotel courtesy bus picked us up early the next morning and ferried us over to terminal two. It was one of those overcast winter days with thick grey clouds smothering the entire northwest region. In just over twelve hours we would be basking in Florida sunshine. As we walked through the sliding doors we were greeted by an immense hive of activity. Line after line of travellers stood in queues that stretched the entire length of the terminal concourse. We joined the back of a very long queue that led to the Delta Airline check in desk. We watched patiently as the queue of people ahead of us slowly dispersed. With small steps we continued to edge towards the check in desk. We started to become aware of people walking away in tears clutching sheets of paper and it wasn't long before news filtered down the queue. It turned out that JFK was expecting blizzard conditions within the next eight hours, and it would not be accepting any flights. A representative of Celebrity cruises appeared at the desk to explain there were no seats available on any other direct flights to Miami. 'What do we do now?' asked one woman in floods of tears as we gathered together in a small group waiting for advice. 'Go home,' replied the rep. He said it in such a cold calculated way that tears erupted from many people who were waiting for a small glimmer of hope. Some unfortunate families had already been through this exact scenario two weeks earlier and this was the second time they'd been let down. When all hope was certifiably lost, we dragged our suitcases across the icy pavements back to the hotel. We drove home, back to North Wales, stunned and depressed and to an empty fridge. It's not always doom and gloom in contrast to this disappointment we experienced the complete opposite when we flew to Australia. In the hotel the night before the flight we had realised that we hadn't printed off our boarding passes. In the lobby of the hotel there was a computer that for the cost of one great British pound you were able to print off your boarding passes. After a few heated arguments and the loss of eight pounds the reception kindly printed them off for us for free. When we finally got to the front of the Cathay Pacific check in desk, a woman took our names then our boarding passes and promptly tore them in half. I wanted to give her a volley of abuse for her blatant disregard of what had effectively cost us an hour of keyboard and printing frustration. All I could see was eight-pound coins tumbling into her wastepaper basket. 'Mr and Mrs Gallagher please wait here, there is someone who would like to speak to you,' the lady with the painted-on smile swivelled on her chair back towards her monitor. Is that it I remember thinking. 'What lady,' I whispered to my wife shrugging my shoulders? In no time at all a smartly dressed woman appeared in a sleek green Cathay Pacific suit, who smiled and asked us to confirm our names. She effortlessly carried an air of seniority, and her approach was built on years of experience in customer service. 'You're travelling to Australia, yes?' I didn't see this as a positive beginning and started blurting out how we had booked these tickets over a year ago. There was a glint in her eye as she explained how Cathay Pacific had over booked our flight to Australia and that she had an offer for us. 'How would you like get to Australia six hours early?' We were then offered £400 to fly on a slightly later flight via Qatar on Qatar Airlines. We were also given £25 of Costa vouchers and a £100 dollar voucher to spend on the flight. It was a great deal, the type you hear about but thought it only happened to other people. We took the offer and arrived in Australia six hours early as promised and yes, I did ask for business class but apparently it was full. I absolutely detest airports as there are so many things that can go wrong, but on this occasion, it finally went right. Sadly, for us these occasions are far and few between, more often than not it's the unexpected that seems to creep up on us.

While waiting to board an Emirates flight to Dubai one year we were told that the tail rudder of our aircraft was buggered, not in those exact words, but technically speaking we grasped the situation. In unison, dozens of passengers let out a huge sigh of dissatisfaction like a gospel choir singing the blues. You could almost hear, 'never mind our safety let us on the plane we don't care that it will go around in circles forever.' An announcement was made by a softly spoken crew member that a new flight was available at another check in desk but there was only limited seating available. The new check in desk happened to be on the other side of the airport and within seconds a stampede broke out. It was carnage as people fell over their own cabin baggage and dragged their children into what was effectively a free for all. Prams and wheelchairs raced alongside each other with the occupants and pushers staring at each other snarling and bearing teeth. Those of us at the back of the gathering were given a head start and we were lucky enough to get to the other desk ahead of the majority of other desperate passengers and get booked onto the next flight. The stragglers unfortunately had to leave on a flight at four in the morning the next day.

Generally, it must be said, that us brits are polite and dignified when it comes to queuing. Americans in my experience don't like to queue for anything they just walk to the front. Our civilised 'after you,' works well for us. We let people with a handful of items go ahead of us at the supermarket checkout.

We open the door for each other knowing that the person we're doing it for will probably get served before us. We get on the plane in an orderly fashion too. 'Can the people in rows thirty to fifty please come forward with your passport in hand.' We accept this willingly. Of course, it makes sense to fill the back of the plane first, after ensuring that our first class and business class are already seated with a glass of Prosecco. Back in cattle class the log jam is down to one family who still can't decide who's sitting next to the window. Then there's Dave, Dave wants to squeeze his oversized hand luggage into the compartment over his seat. It doesn't fit, but he's prepared to punch it in to place like a heavy weight prize fighter. Dave's wearing his DJ white headphones which means he doesn't need to acknowledge the rest of humanity. The flight attendant taps him lightly on the shoulder being careful not induce 'air rage,' as it's known or technically speaking as we're still on the ground 'cabin rage.' He looks at her dumbfounded and says, 'it fitted in last time, din it?' Another member of the flight crew tries to tell Dave to use another locker, but it falls on deaf ears as track three starts with 'i predict a Riot,' by the Kaiser chiefs. When everybody has finally wedged themselves into place and buckled up, the doors are locked, and we happily set off to the skies above. Isn't it strange when you arrive at your destination that everybody all stands up at once? The cabin crew have gone into hiding and none of them would dream of saying, stay in your seat and we will call out which rows can get off first. Yes, you will hear the announcement, 'please stay in your seat (click) and keep your (click) seatbelt (click) fastened and wait until the plane has (click click click) come to a stop, thank you.' The overhead lockers start springing open all over the plane, because people need to get their luggage down first. At this point no one gives a flying fuck for anyone its 'Squid Game.' Dave's got the 'Eye of the Tiger,' rocking in both ear drums and he plans to get down the aisle like he going to score a try for England. The lineout can be agitated by the smallest hold up and the mindset is that no one gives way to no one. While standing in the twisted pose executed by the wonderful John Hurt as elephant man, I get a chance to glare at the kid called Oliver who has kicked the bag of my chair for a full five hours. Oliver is not fazed by my best impersonation of Tony Soprano and my hardest look of scorn which quickly turns to a smile as his mother stares at me. The guy who squashed my head by reclining his chair as I looked out of the window before we took off is now staring at me with the same stare, I gave Oliver. Who the fuck reclines their chair before take-off? My wife had slapped him on the back of his head to make him put his chair back up to stop my skull from being cracked open like a walnut. He never argued or complained so thankfully it didn't turn into one of those moments you see on social media. Air rage is now a common phrase in the aviation industry, but I doubt it even existed before the nineties. With alcohol fuelled hen and stag parties becoming more common place and the claustrophobic seating space now afforded to travellers, it's no wonder that all hell breaks out every now and then. There are horrific stories on the internet of people going off their rocker just because they were refused another Gin and Tonic. If I could change one aspect of flying it would be to put a ban on alcohol. I'd find a way of cleanly and quickly breathalysing passengers before letting them on the plane. I wouldn't serve alcohol on the plane and Id stop serving it in airport lounges. I like a beer like most people and love that holiday feeling of chilling in a bar before taking to the skies. But the evidence is more than compelling when it comes to the reasons why someone would want to attack other passengers or threaten the flight attendant. In some cases, there have been incidents of air rage were a drunken passenger wants to open the door at thirty thousand feet. Sometimes I'd like to open the door for them. I often wonder what reaction those same people would have if they saw the pilot and crew sitting at the bar? Recently a twenty-eight-year-old guy in China was arrested for throwing coins into the engine of a plane as he was climbing the stairs to get on board. This apparently is a Chinese custom to bring good luck. It happened in February 2019 at Anqing Tianzhushan airport, and the plane was part of the budget airline called 'Lucky Air.' The not so lucky passenger was fined heavily.

It's not just some tosser that can stop you getting off the ground another sure-fire way to stay on the ground is to accuse someone of acting suspiciously. It was during one of our many holidays to Turkey that we found ourselves in a bit of turbulence before we'd even took off. We were heading home after spending yet another marvellous week in the pretty coastal resort of Icmeler. Having boarded our return flight at Dalaman airport with no fuss, we became aware that something was causing some tension with the crew. The boarding process had seemed nothing out of the unusual and i could see no reason why our flight to Manchester wouldn't depart on time. My wife and i were sat near to the aircraft door and it soon became apparent that there were some hushed tones of a suppressed argument taking place right in front of us. Blocking the doorway and access to the interior of the plane were two flight attendants accompanied by the captain. In front of them stood two tall thin men dressed in what I believe to be called a Pahalgam. They both possessed well established beards and each with a turban like hat. This unfortunately was not the most popular choice of fashion during the time as the search for Osama Bin Ladin was still at its highest. Wearing a baseball cap doesn't make you a boy racer or having two mobile phones doesn't mean you're a drug dealer either. If I wear a suit it can narrow people's perceptions. If you knew me but hadn't seen me in a suit before you might wonder if I'm due in court? Or am i attending an interview, a wedding, a christening? If it's a black suit it's a funeral. I once tried to change a pair of shoes I'd purchased while wearing my scruffy ripped work clothes, the store assistant in customer services flatly refused as I had no receipt. I returned wearing a suit and they offered to change them or give me my money back no questions asked?

'Why are we not allowed on the plane,' asked one of the tall gentlemen? Agitated and understandably upset they looked beyond the crew and in my direction. 'Someone has said you were acting suspiciously,' replied the captain apologetically. 'Who is this person who condemns us I want to know? I will accuse them of acting suspiciously as well.' I could see the blood drain from the captain's face as he heard the retaliation. 'Please don't do that, we will need to take everybody off the plane if you make that accusation and no one will get home. The security team are on their way here now to assist.' The captain still maintained his position with his arms stretched across the portal of the door. Behind him standing resolute were his stewards and now the co-pilot. Other passengers had noticed the presence of the Captain and his Co-pilot, and the atmosphere of the plane started to change from loud chatter to low conversations. Just as the stand-off was becoming almost too embarrassing to watch a Turkish security person arrived. He seemed out of breath but managed to wave a clip board in the air in order to get the captains attention. He pushed between the two men standing at the doorway and like a judge summing up a murder case he gave his verdict. 'We've checked the luggage over and over, it's all clear, he gasped. Background checks complete no concerns they're good to go.' There was no time for any further discussion, the captain moved out of the way instantly and apologised once more. 'You can make an official complaint when you land, but for now please say nothing more.' He was almost pleading as he gave his advice, but never stayed to hear any further responses. The so called suspicious gentlemen took their seats which were situated only a few rows behind me to my left. I watched as a man stood up to let them take the two seats nearest the window. All through this unfolding drama I had become fixated with the old brown leather briefcase that one of the men were carrying. It looked like the briefcase the Chancellor of the exchequer carries to the budget. It just wasn't the kind of luggage you see anyone carrying on a plane. It certainly wasn't the type of thing you'd put your Pringles and cheese sandwiches in. There wasn't much conversation taking place and we were now at a volume otherwise known as squeaky bum time or dead silent. I felt like I was part of a u boat crew in the Second World War, waiting for depth chargers to blow us to kingdom come. That was one of the longest journeys I've ever made. Four hours waiting to hear the locks click open from that old briefcase was mental torture. A bomb, a gun, a prawn sandwich or a copy of the Manchester Evening news? God only knows what was in there but imagine if their accuser was right all along? This is what the fear of flying does to you. It turned out that the only person who was trying to kill us was the pilot, who landed the plane at such a steep angle and at such a speed that we nearly didn't make the turn at the end of the runway. The funny thing was the guys who'd had trouble getting on the plane were terrified by the pilot's landing skills and I could see them looking nervously at each other.

It's a good job they weren't on the outward journey to Turkey one week earlier because the landing at Manchester was a walk in the park compared to the landing in Turkey. The weather was so bad as we flew over Turkey that I had forgotten it was a daytime flight. Pre-occupied, i had failed to notice that the sky surrounding us had slowly turned pitch black. Flashes of light sporadically lit up the darkness and at first i didn't quite grasp the situation. There was no sound accompanying this humidity infused light show and there was no turbulence or the jolts that you see people endure in disaster movies. To be honest it wasn't until the captain announced that he had already made two attempts to land that I realised i was engulfed in my worst nightmare. The pilot announced that this was going to be his third and final attempt to put us down safely in Dalaman and if this failed, we were to head off to another airport. I had been engrossed in a movie and took little notice when we'd been politely asked to fasten our seatbelts. When suddenly realising the situation, I left George Clooney and his fishing boat as I was now in my own perfect storm. I was getting a real sinking feeling which was best described as sudden vertical drops that took your breath away. Your stomach becomes detached from the rest of your body and tries to make a break for freedom using your mouth as the escape hatch. The landing gear clunks into place which allows for some optimism, and you can hear the whirling sound of gears rotating as the flaps on the wings tilt down to push us towards our destination. Our arrival into Dalaman airport is heralded by the thump of the wheels meeting the tarmac. Even sitting in a chair, it feels like a body blow from a boxer to the lower abdomen, but it's more than welcome. As we alighted the plane, I could see that the afternoon sky was still in recovery from the midst of darkness. The airport was lit as you would expect it to be in the later evening with the runway lights gleaming far into the distance. Forks of lightening were splitting the horizon in every direction, and they seemed to linger an extra second or two as if waiting to be photographed in all their splendour. It took little imagination to think of some angry Greek God standing above the clouds hurling bolts of electricity to punish the puny mortals below. Looking at this from the relative safety of earth and not out of a little window at ten thousand feet made me realise just how precarious our situation had been. By the time we had picked up our luggage and got through passport control the sky was miraculously blue with hardly a cloud in sight. Figures state that the earth has on average two thousand thunderstorms raging around the planet at any given time. Apparently most commercial aircraft will get hit more than once a year but with today's technology it causes no concern. Try telling that to the 81 passengers heading to Baltimore on a Pan Am flight in 1963. This was the last airline crash attributed to a lightning strike, but from where I was sitting, we could have been the next.

CHAPTER 8

The Road to Masca

I passed my driving test at the age of twenty-eight and although late by some standards I certainly made up for it. My only experience of driving up until then was dumper trucks and forklifts. I'd say i was a good driver and with thirty years behind me without a scrape I'd say that probably qualifies me as better than average. I was always the designated driver on golfing trips to Spain, my mates stated that I had an advantage because I was left-handed. When they were downing pints of cold beer after walking four miles in the sun, I'd be drinking a shandy, where's the left handed advantage in that? My experience of driving abroad started when the kids were only toddlers, I'd hire the cheapest car that I could afford and drive them up into the mountains of Lanzarote. Our first trip was to Teguise market, which was situated well above sea level and certainly tested the gear box of our over used Fiat Panda. This was a car that was realistically designed to go to the corner shop and back and could be easily swallowed up by a small pothole in the road. We would shout fight and argue wherever we travelled by car with my daughter wedged between the two boys in a constant battle of sibling rivalry and name calling. This never caused me to lose concentration because when the squabbling became louder so did the radio. I could probably be compared to Goofy in one of those old Disney cartoons where you would see him driving along a treacherous mountain side road oblivious to any danger. With a slack jawed hillbilly laugh I'd tell the kids to take in the marvellous views while threatening them with the 'no pocket money' clause. This can be found in the book, 'Acceptable Bribery, for Parents.' In hindsight these trips would have been far safer if I had of purchased the hotel's family coach trip, which included a market visit and wine tasting. The problem was their extortionate rates, which were usually the equivalent of three days car hire. In order to save a few quid, id' opt for Pedro's 'Carmageddon Car hire.' Oh, how i loved that smug feeling when we'd bump into another family from our complex who'd say they hadn't seen us on the coach. 'That's because we've hired a car and it cost me less than your coach trip,' this was all done with the good grace of a smug, tight arsed penny pincher. I'd point over to our mustard-coloured death trap with the broken air conditioning like I was pointing at a Bentley. 'We're just getting off from here to explore the rest of the island,' I'd say this with an arrogant whiff of coolness. This was an immense porkie on two accounts. The first being, that after one day of heart stopping near misses and the occasional swerve from an oncoming lorry, I'd swear I'd never drive abroad again. The hire car usually stayed parked up outside the hotel until it needed to be returned. On the way home from Teguise market I had taken a wrong turn that ultimately tested my nerve and driving skills to their limits. After traipsing around the market, we headed back to the resort driving through what was effectively low cloud. Teguise sits two hundred and twenty metres above sea level and is prone to collecting a mass of what are known as Lenticular clouds. They hover like a spaceship, heavy with moisture and shroud the hillside from the outside world. We drove straight into them and began a steep descent cutting nervously through the dense mist. The kids thought it was funny and laughed as they detected the nervousness in my onboard commentary. 'Dad can't see a thing right now it's like I'm flying a plane with a blindfold on. Only one bloody windscreen wiper working and it's on your mums' side.' With obscured vision I could just make out a sign offering a left turn. The slip road demanded a tight left turn and looked to be taking us in the direction of the coastal town of 'Costa Teguise.' I could just make out the chevrons as we turned onto a narrow slip of tarmac which quickly turned into a loose gravel road. Suddenly the car started to lurch and jump at the front end and the steering started to feel like someone else had their hands on it. The dense cloud began to disperse and within seconds we broke through into the bright sun light. It was like the moment when Dorothy Gale arrived in the land of Oz, and everything went Technicolour. I had turned onto a road that was leading down to a working quarry. No ordinary quarry, I'm talking a gigantic hole in the ground type quarry with a steep rocky road leading to its base. From my wife's viewpoint there was nothing to her right only a sheer drop into oblivion. I had no choice but to continue as a three point turn even in a Fiat Panda would be near impossible and too risky with the kids in the back. In front of me was an empty wagon kicking up dust clouds as it made its way down into the quarry basin to be reloaded. The Pandas fifteen-inch wheels were climbing over small rocks and boulders and all I could think about was how the hell do I get back out of here. I'd decided that I had no choice but to get down to the level that was last seen in prehistoric times and do a u turn. It took some time, but we finally levelled out in front of a fleet of huge lorries and bulldozers with their drivers staring at us in disbelief. The tyres on these machines were as big as our hire car. I half expected to see Fred Flintstone sitting on a Brontosaurus. Lathered in extra sweat, i smiled and calmly turned around like a tugboat in front of a cruise ship. Maybe I didn't smile, but either way I began to pray that we didn't meet one of these monster trucks on our way back up the hill. The thought of having to reverse back down was unthinkable. As luck would have it, we made it back to the main road and a short time later back to our hotel. The car was now the colour of whitish grey or perhaps 'Ochre' depending on if you work in B&Q. It was coated in a thick paste of dust particles which had stuck like glue due to the damp precipitation off the low-level clouds. These were the days before car hire companies got their reputation for trying to rip off holiday makers. Nowadays you must photograph the vehicle like a vogue model before you drive to avoid getting charged for damages that were already there. Most of the cars you hired back then were already in poor condition to begin with and as long as you brought it back with four wheels and windows intact, they were happy.   I think i probably exceeded their expectations when I returned this Fiat Panda actually looking like a Panda.' The landscape of Lanzarote ensured that most vehicles were inevitably treated to a jet wash before their next outing, but my return would have prompted some serious sponging and overtime. For over thirty years I've took my chances behind the wheel in cities, towns and mountains and found none of them any more stressful than driving through London. That is except one particular place, Masca. Hidden away in the southwest corner of Tenerife is a road that winds its way across a range of high mountains. My wife and I had decided to circumnavigate the edge of Tenerife for a change of scenery. Heading anti clockwise we set off from Costa Adeje and headed towards Santa Cruz by joining the TF1 . The main roads of Tenerife are very well maintained and the roads running through villages are kept to an exceedingly high standard. Once we had passed the airport, I realised that we were now heading into unfamiliar territory. The TF1 which is the main motorway that stretches 103 kilometres from El Moledo to Santa Cruz is best described for most part as a dual carriageway. One thing I've come to accept when driving anywhere home or abroad is it's always the driver that misses anything remotely interesting. Passengers seem to take great delight in pointing out the things that is impossible to see from behind the wheel. 'Oh my god look at that amazing house on the side of that mountain it must have cost millions.' To which I reply sarcastically 'sorry I'm driving and currently concentrating on the back of this massive lorry carrying toxic waste from radioactiveville.' Undeterred and unworried by a possible collision with two hundred drums of sulphuric acid my wife will continue to convey even more key information that I'm missing. 'They have beautiful pink curtains and a statue of a whale in the front garden. No sorry it's not a whale it's one of those sword fishy things.' Meanwhile I take my chance to get beyond this toxic truck of doom and overtake it by flooring the accelerator of our 1.2 Vauxhall Opal until it screams in pain. 'You mean Swordfish,' I say, breathing out a sigh of relief as the truck moves away in my rear-view mirror. 'Actually, it might have been a dolphin I'm not sure,' says my wife.

'If we get lost, I'll remember those curtains, that way we will know we're heading back in the right direction.' To be fair, my wife has rescued us with this tactic before. On many occasions she has assured me that we are heading in the right direction due to the fact she remembers a feature of somebody's house. 'Terrible door and it needs painting.'

Santa Cruz the capitol of Tenerife was to be a fleeting visit. It would be fair to say that I've spent more time in a McDonald's drive through than I did driving through Santa Cruz. This is something I now deeply regret having read its astonishing history. Considered by the Guardian newspapers as one of the top twelve places to live in the world, it's no wonder Lord Admiral Nelson was keen to overthrow it back in 1797. Most brits end up legless in Tenerife, Nelson however became armless as he landed on the beach at Paso Alto. Hit by grape shot from a cannon he parted company with his right arm which was famously amputated later that day. Nowadays he'd be more likely to be hit on the beach by club reps offering him free shots. It wasn't long before we found ourselves on a road that was to take us high over the Parque Rural de Anaga mountains. It was a road like nothing we had driven on before and it was to prepare us for what was to come later that day. Surrounded by dense forests and sweeping deep canyons it was a road that had scenery that was breath-taking and exhilarating all in one. I'd never driven at such an altitude and part of the excitement was not knowing where we were going or where we'd end up. We never felt in any danger as the road was wide enough for two vehicles and we were overtaken several times by more confident drivers who i guessed must have been local. I'm no slouch when it comes to pushing through the gears but I'm hesitant if I don't know the route. Some people flew past us at ridiculous speeds on bends that I thought would launch them into gods waiting room. Vans went past us like they had just plummeted through some time traveling worm hole. Some of these cars and vans looked like they were from decades ago, a Morris Minor Traveller complete with wooden trim blew a cloud of smoke from its exhaust as it sped past with a nineteen sixties number plate. Chickens in wire cages were tied to its roof and slid from side to side with the vehicle's momentum. Two black Labradors stared out of the back window oblivious to the risks that their owners next turn could bring. The driver had the look of a man well into his late seventies dishevelled with swept back long grey hair and a cigarette hanging casually from his bottom lip. A weather-beaten face peered over the steering wheel and the last thing on his mind was the Highway Code. He had probably seen his fair share of nervous tourists to realise that it worked out to be far less risky to dice with death than it was to be sat crawling behind an indecisive moron who normally drives on the left-hand side of the road. Eventually, as is always the case we started our decent down the mountain side into a town that, until we seen a road sign didn't know existed. Punta Del Hidalgo translated using Google means 'Tip of the Gentleman,' make of that what you willy. A hidden resort with only a few hotels and restaurants. It was probably a bolt hole for the people of Santa Cruz. It had a beautiful lido which was spotlessly clean with ladders that dropped from the pool side into the unprotected coves of clear blue sea water. We stopped for a few hours and swam in the chilled water of the lido before surrendering to a cold beer in gardens of the hotel bar Angeleco which was adjacent to where we had parked.

We resisted the temptation to stay for longer and headed off towards the next town and with the intention of finding a road that would take us in a homeward direction. We had seen on our map that the TF5 ran from the town of San Cristobal de la Laguna to Puerto de la Cruz which looked to be our best route home. When we did eventually find the motorway, we made the decision to bypass Puerto de la Cruz as we were now getting to the point, we're being lost again wasn't so appealing. We continued along the TF5 keeping the views of the famous mount Teide on our left-hand side. Somehow, we managed to miss a vital slip road that would have taken us directly towards Adeje and kept us on the good side of the mountain range of Teno. I can't tell you the reason why, but we continued to follow the road to the far western corner of Tenerife, to the outskirts of a town called Buenavista. Due to the temperature starting to rise inside and outside of the car we decided to pull up at a drab looking roadside café.

This crumbling oasis in the middle of nowhere was detached from any other buildings and had last seen a lick of paint when the Titanic was launched. Straight out of a spaghetti western three men dressed in working clothes sat on a wooden veranda sipping beers watching my every step. I sauntered across the shingle car park trying to give the impression of a man that just might be able to handle himself in a gun fight.' Actually, i had a pair of beige shorts and flip flops on my feet so i don't think they were intimidated whatsoever. The café interior was bleak with flaking whitewashed walls and a ceiling straddled with thick wooden beams. The remnants of some torn Christmas decorations or decorations from a local fiesta were still hanging loosely from the joists and danced in unison to the breeze of a solitary ceiling fan. I took two bottles of water from a well-stocked fridge and while paying took the opportunity to ask for directions. The woman behind the counter shrugged her shoulders and shook her head but smiled as I handed over a couple of Euros. There were no other people inside the last chance saloon, so I had no choice but to approach the tabasco triplets outside. I stood holding two bottles of water sweating in the heat of the midday sun. Looking at my attire and sunglasses they would have already guessed why I was approaching. 'Perdon Senor's tu es donde Playa Las Americas?' Not the best Spanish they'd ever heard but at least one of them nodded and replied in some broken English. 'From here is left to end of road.' He circled with his finger to explain a roundabout. You is far to go over, how you say grande, er, beeg montanas, Masca, Masca. Ees not so safe from this place. Maybe you wish to go how you say alrededor, er longer mas' road?' I kind of got the gist of his friendly directions and I thanked him with my best scouse 'gracias,' and got back in the car. 'I think there are two ways home,' I explained to my wife pointing through the windscreen, 'back, over those mountains or back the way we came.' We both quenched our thirst before simultaneously saying 'mountains.' Ten minutes later we came across a road sign that was in Spanish and English that resembled the small print on an insurance form with a Union Jack symbol. *Masca – You take this road at your own risk. Falling rocks.'*

We looked up at the mountain range in front of us and were not too intimidated by the climb that lay ahead. I think above all we wanted to embrace the adventure and convinced ourselves that it could not be any more difficult than the journey over the de Anaga mountains earlier this morning. Before setting off I noticed a communications tower at the highest point of the mountain range and said to my wife, 'as long as we don't end up there.' An hour later we passed that communications tower with our nerves completely torn to shreds. The road to Masca was littered with tight hairpin bends and terrifying cliff edges. The only vehicles we met were from head on and never from behind. The road was wide enough for only one vehicle, but wisely some passing places had been incorporated along the entire route. The occasional car never caused too much of a problem and by tucking in your wing mirrors you could pass each other with millimetres to spare. When the local bus came hurtling down the hill like it was being driven by Sandra Bullock and Keanu Reeves the blood drained from my face. Instead of a Hollywood actor behind the wheel it was Manuel Gears' the local bus companies pot head. He had made this journey umpteen times and with a quick smoke before setting off it never bothered him a bit. He had timed his meeting with us perfectly and passed us with his arm hanging out of the window and Bob Marley telling him not to worry about a thing blaring out of his window. As we passed the communication tower Id mentioned earlier our ears were popping frantically and we were close to synchronised nose bleeds. The downhill journey seemed far easier with more stretches of straight road and less lethal bends. If the journey hadn't been difficult enough, my wife had somehow messed with the cars de misters and somehow managed to induce an environment of dense fog that took an absolute age to clear from the windscreen. This would bring about a loud heated conversation of foul language with me explaining that taking a hair pin bend with the equivalent of having cataracts is a fucking death wish. The sat nag, as I call her is the reason for multiple wrong turnings over the years, but she is always the calmest in difficult situations. As we entered Costa Adeje and got back to the gentler familiar streets the relief washed over me. My wife doesn't drive so it's hard to explain that there is some immense pressure involved when driving abroad. The car however certainly understood exactly what we'd been through as it had a burnt black oil stripe from the bonnet right along the side of the car. It had melted into the paintwork. This would mean I'd have to put on an act and say to the car hire people they had given me a dodgy motor, otherwise just like Nelson, my trip to Santa Cruz would also end up costing me and arm and a leg.

Back in the seventies a singer by the name of Jim Croce released a song called 'Time in a Bottle,' and it became a big hit.

It had lyrics that must have resonated with so many people.

If I could make days last forever
If words could make wishes come true
I'd save every day like a treasure and then again, I would spend them with you.

Time shouldn't be kept in a bottle it should be spent creating as many memories as you can gather.

Even if it is just for a day driving a dodgy car up a mountain it will be time well spent. The only thing you should do with a bottle is drink its contents and say cheers. One of my favourite sayings is, *'I'd rather have a bottle in front of me than a frontal lobotomy.'*

CHAPTER 9

Is There a Doctor Onboard?

If I could afford to travel business class, I would. It must be an amazing experience, although a costly one. It's not the quaffing of Champagne or the better-quality food that appeals to me, not at all. What I want is the ability to lie down horizontal and sleep all the way to my destination. When travelling in 'sardine class,' if you do manage to fall asleep by some miracle, your chin will need to rest unnaturally on your chest. Your head has no choice but to roll about like a marble balanced on tea tray. Some people by those wrap around horseshoe shaped pillows and i can't believe they offer anything other than a bit of neck support. It's the equivalent of putting a brush handle down the back of a Queens guard and saying, 'there you go that'll help you stand up straight for eight hours.' At some point you will jolt and lift your head up quickly and look at the people around you with drool dripping from the side of your mouth. It's a form of torture that you see in a war film where an exhausted prisoner is repeatedly questioned during sleep deprivation. We call it a holiday. Just as you find that comfortable position where you've lost all feeling in your left leg from the hip down and your right foot is touching the other passengers foot beneath their seat, an announcement blares out. A muffled voice tells you 'We have scratch cards for sale, and you can win a luxury holiday for two, probably to the same bloody place you're flying to. Then a little time later just when you finally drop off, another announcement blares out, offering items from the inflight magazine. Then another shout out for your spare change for charity. If by some miracle you have got yourself into a deep sleep and you're flying to the USA, don't worry you're going to get a visa to complete onboard. Suddenly it's a busman's holiday as you now start to fill in forms. On long haul destinations, passengers are given a complimentary, tongue blistering, vacuum packed meal. Containing all the nutrition of a toasted sock you tuck in gratefully. This tasty treat must be eaten while you impersonate a Tyrannosaurus Rex and shorten your arms to half their length. The remnants of this high-flying culinary disaster, stay on your drop-down tray for the next hour until a glamorous refuse collector squash it back on to the trolley.

So it is with absolute gratitude that I thank the designers of the two tiered A380. This humongous flying beast of the aviation world has taken pity on those in the cheap seats. It's a delight in every sense of the word and a long-haul flight becomes so much more bearable. I've travelled on this aircraft a few times and I've enjoyed every minute of it. During 2020 we travelled from Manchester to Thailand via Dubai, both legs of the journey were onboard an A380. We had pre booked two seats on the upper deck due to the fact we were setting off straight from work and thought that twin seats would offer us a better chance of relaxation. It was around eight o'clock in the evening when we climbed into the skies above Manchester along with the smoothest of take offs that I now associate with this aircraft. As it happened to be an evening flight the lights on board were dimmed and most people had quickly settled into a film. I'm not sure how far thirty minutes gets you in an A380, but I estimated we were somewhere over the Norfolk coastline and heading towards Northern Europe. From the central seating area a few rows behind us, a sudden scream for help caught most people's attention. I hadn't put my headphones on at this point, so the high pitched shriek of a woman's voice easily broke the gentle humming sound of the engines. Make of that what you will. The cry for help escalated and possibly due to the world we now live in, my immediate thought was 'terrorist.' My instant reaction was to stand up and see what was causing this commotion. A woman who was stood between a row of four seats, looked to be wrestling with a man sat next to her. She shook him violently and I could see that he looked pale and almost lifeless. He had fixated eyes and would not have looked out of place in Madam Tussauds. He skin colour matched his grey hair and he was now frothing at the mouth. Surely, I'm not going to be doing CPR for a third time and on a plane of all places. Nobody moved a muscle and to be honest i was a little dumbstruck myself. As luck would have it the man sitting in the seat in front of me turned out to be a doctor. The crew where quickly on the scene and in no time at all they were handing the doctor a bottle of oxygen with a mask attached to it. The woman began to explain to all around her that her husband had been complaining of chest pains earlier that day. An announcement came across the PA asking if there was a doctor on board, which i thought was peculiar as a doctor had already come forward? 'Please make yourself known to the cabin crew,' the pilot had requested. Having one doctor sitting near you on a plane when you're in a serious condition is a stroke of luck, but when another doctor appeared from downstairs it must be like winning the lottery.

I can't get an appointment at my local doctor's surgery, unless I know that I'm going to be sick three weeks in advance, this guy gets two doctors come to him on a plane. My dad is eighty nine and his doctor will not do home visits. Maybe I should take him on a plane? They also managed to move the sick guy and his wife to another part of the plane with more room to stabilise. Probably business class where he could lie down. Mmm, I could pull this off with a glass of frothing Andrew's liver salts, sorry bad taste. I figured that we may have to land somewhere like Heathrow or Gatwick or even Amsterdam to get this chap to a hospital for treatment. It became evident that he must have recovered well enough to continue and completed the journey to Dubai as we heard nothing more regarding the matter. However, Lady Luck wasn't completely on his side as we discovered on our approach to Dubai.

Somewhere over Dubai our pilot made announcement that took

us all by surprise. 'Ladies and gentlemen due to unforeseen circumstances we will be delayed for quite some time due to a high degree of flooding at our destination. We have been asked to take a holding pattern until we are given instructions to land. Currently there is only one runway operating at the airport and this is causing a backlog of take-off and landings.' Dubai as you will probably know sits in the Arabian dessert and seldom sees any rain and it can be years before a real downpour occurs. It's forty degrees centigrade down there, nearly as hot as a McDonald's tea. I looked out of the window and to my absolute horror watched another aircraft above us turning tightly to one side and dropping towards the tail of our plane. We were surrounded by a spiral of other aircraft which filled the sky in every direction. I felt like I'd suddenly joined the Red Arrows as we continued to turn into the same tight circle that was creating something like one of those solar system mobiles where the earth and Uranus spins around the sun. In this case, Uranus was twitching and spinning high around the Earth. An hour later we splashed down on to a flooded Dubai runway with spray streaking across the windows like we'd entered a giant car wash. It then took us just under an hour to find a parking space. It was like Asda on a Christmas Eve, there were no trolleys left and the airport terminal was rammed in every direction. The fiasco continued as this is a 'silent' airport, were no PA system announcements are allowed. Every TV screen with flight information showed the same information, delayed was written next to every destination in the world. All the other TV screens told you how great life is with a Rolex watch or that you can now buy the best apartments on the 'Palm' for up to twenty five million pound. We went mad and splashed out some cash on some pastries and two cups of coffee then sat patiently waiting for information. The airport was in chaos, or as someone I once knew pronounced it 'chouse.' Gates were being announced on the boards only to change minutes later causing all the people at gate 3a for Munich to join all the other people at 3b for Zagreb. A few minutes later the boards would announce that the flight for

Zagreb was now leaving from gate 4c and so three hundred people would flock like migrating Wilder beasts to 4c to join three hundred people waiting for a flight to New Delhi. This went on for nearly eight hours before we were finally called to our boarding gate. After being corralled into yet another holding pen, we were finally bussed across the airport to join our aircraft. Crammed together into a claustrophobic atmosphere we watched jealousy as a first-class passenger was taken to the same aircraft alone on a similar bus. Most of us had been watching this chap fall about the airport pissed for the last two hours. The water that had engulfed the airport was still evident in large pools strewn across the airport in all directions. The undercarriage of our plane sat in a shallow pond like a giant Heron about to scoop up a fish. It's good to know that us brits aren't the only people who get caught out by the weather. A couple of flakes of snow or a few leaves on a train track and the UK has a transport melt down. Back in 1960 some apprentice architect may have raised his hand during the planning of the Dubai airport and said, 'what about some emergency drainage?' That person was probably the laughingstock of the office for many years, well not today he wouldn't have been. The rain that fell on our visit was the heaviest rainfall in twenty-six years, January 12th, 2020, saw 7.5 inches of rain. I'm beginning to think it's me. I arrived in New York one Christmas, and it was amazingly warm, while California was knee deep in snow. I turn up in the dessert and it floods. I've sat in Tenerife for seven days under a grey sky in the middle of July were the sun never appeared until i was getting back on the plane. It was so cold you needed a jumper and yet the holiday rep kept telling me to put on the factor fifty. 'There's still harmful UVA rays getting through you know,' she scolded me in a broad Scottish accent. Could she not see that fifty odd people were sitting around the pool hidden inside extra layers of clothing and not a bathing costume or tattoo in sight. We looked like the survivors of a shipwreck huddled together waiting for a hot cup of tea.

CHAPTER 10

Breakaway

The airport is a place where the space time continuum warps into another dimension. Ok I didn't understand that either. I'm no Stephen Hawkins, more of a NVQ in welding type of guy, let me explain. At the time of booking your holiday there is the option of the ten o'clock night flight which is far cheaper than the easy' just after a hearty breakfast flight. There's also the stupid o'clock in the morning flight,' which is far cheaper than the sensible afternoon o'clock flight. Having opted for the super saver class we arrived in the airport long before the first hint of daylight. Basically, sleep walking as you join the queue with all the other 'like-minded' careful spenders. The flight may be at six, but you must be at the airport two hours earlier, something you neglected to consider when booking. Plus, you need to consider the time spent getting out of bed and getting to the airport. The customary argument begins once you've dropped your car off with the 'Gone in Sixty Seconds crew.' These are the people who will drive your car carefully to their off-site car park, otherwise known as farmer Giles potato field.

The lack of sleep fuels the conversation regarding anything from 'you nearly killed us when you hit that kerb,' to the old favourite, 'did you lock the door?' By the time you get past check in and the wonderful chirpy security team, you are the equivalent of the walking dead. The next official task is to check the departures board, only to see no boarding gate listed for your flight yet. That means time is now on your side and a bit of duty-free browsing is now on the agenda. It seems perfectly natural to some people to buy a gigantic Toblerone and a bottle of perfume from the same shop. Not only do I need to own something that could pass as a dangerous triangular cosh, but I must also get a pair of designer sunglasses. The marketing people are hoping it never crossed my mind that I am going on holiday and to take my sunglasses. What about that designer watch? I've never thought about buying a Patek Phillips Nautilus before now and yet now seems the best time to buy time. The price tag of a hundred thousand makes me realise that there's more enjoyment in a Toblerone. By the time you saunter over to the crowded bar to join all the other five am drinkers the concept of time has almost dissolved. Two pints of San Miguel rubber stamps the fact that you're on holiday and the departure board eventually comes back into play. On this occasion we are travelling with my wife's sister and her husband. It's strangely acceptable that the kids are sitting nearby while you knock down a couple of pints and a few Prosecco's, while telling them to behave themselves as they slide across the windows facing the runway. The flight, I recall was uneventful and four hours later we were shuffling wearily through Tenerife South airport.

Waiting for the suitcases to appear on to the carousel is a pet hate of mine. Someone's suitcase has to be last off the plane and there are many times I've stood there with other stragglers sweating with fear. Most of the other passengers have long gone and a single suitcase has been going around in circles without no takers since your arrival. You study it and start thinking 'I wonder if it's full of drugs and the security team are waiting to pounce on the collector?' Eventually and much to your relief your case appears from the bowels of hell, tangled up with a long-forgotten Pram from a previous flight. You thank God and the baggage handler that you now don't have to go shopping for new underpants, clothes and a toothbrush. We now make our way to bus stop 3b and introduce ourselves to Senor Miguel the bus driver who is neither happy nor sad to see us. It seems by his relaxed swagger that he has all the time in the world. He's a big guy in his fifties who can lift a suitcase like a he's swinging a feather duster. His greying beard and moustache plus rotund features give him the look of Orson Welles, except a cigarette hangs loosely from his lips instead of a cigar. We took our seats two thirds of the way down the coach and let the air conditioning blow our cares away. It was still early morning, but the humidity was all too evident. There are pretentious smiles through gritted teeth from the other passengers who'd boarded the coach nearly an hour ago. As with the last suitcase syndrome there's also some people who will be dropped off last at their hotel. It all depends on the route map and Senor Miguel's wife. Is he going shopping after work or going to meet the other drivers at Don Pedro's tapas bar? Ten minutes from the airport the air brakes go on and we make our first stop outside a small hotel reception. We are on a Main Street and the coach is unable to park near the kerb. 'La Cockeroacha Casa,' shouts the driver and a disappointed couple make their way down the aisle. We all stare at the miserable looking couple through the coach windows thinking the same thing, 'thank fuck were not staying at that hell hole.' The driver drops their cases to the pavement and stares at them while holding out his arm as if to give directions towards the reception. His open hand remains filled with fresh air as the couple turn towards the hotel that doesn't match the brochure and he prepares for seven days of 'i can't believe you picked this place. ' Even in the poorly lit hallway we can clearly see the tension as once again the air brakes signal our departure. The next hotel has a good-sized car park and a family of five depart the coach and are warmly greeted by a door person who is ready to collect their baggage. You get the feeling that they've stayed here before as the kids run straight through the huge glass covered reception to stand near a beautiful shimmering pool surrounded by the strategically placed palms. The next destination takes us up a very steep and winding hill. It's away from the main resort and looks to be a more executive area. The street lighting looks new and the manicured lawns either side of the road are so lush that they could be mistaken for artificial grass. The coach reached the brow of the hill effortlessly and then nose dives into a steep angle facing the distant bay of Los Christianos. The early morning sun creates reflections of glistening lights that skip across the harbour like sparkling diamonds.   The excitement of the journey had long worn off and the thought of getting some catchup sleep was all that mattered.   Ahead of us, were more hotel stops and then when we eventually get to our own hotel there will be the checking of the passports and all the other usual formalities. As I pondered on how many hours there are in a day I slipped into a dreamlike state where reality and imagination become entwined for fleeting moments. One second, you're on a bus seat and the next your sat at a bar with Homer Simpson and Frank Sinatra. A sudden jerk of the bus wakes me from my slumber. I lift my head up wearily and I realise that the bus has moved forward by a short distance, maybe a yard or so. Out of my window to the side I can see the panels of the bus hydraulically lifted to allow access to the luggage hold. The last time I had seen the driver he was getting off the bus. I had fallen asleep before he'd got back on the bus, thus creating a bit of a time lapse. Unbeknown to me the departing family had been given their cases by the driver and had disappeared into their new residence. Frantically I assessed the situation, the coach had suddenly moved without the driver or so I assumed. The first ten rows of seats were taken up by some elderly people which made me think that none of them would be agile enough to spring up out of their chair and steer the bus. Oh my god why is everyone so calm, where's Sandra Bullock when you need her? I had to act quickly and so I jumped up and hurtled down the aisle. In a flash I gave myself instructions to steer the coach down the hill until I can somehow locate the handbrake. It was like the Matrix; I was moving faster than all those around me. That was until I came face to face with the driver who was staring at his phone and then at me in one swift movement.

'Que estas haciendo?' A tight smile and a flash of teeth beneath his moustache hid his confused expression.

'What am I doing?' Good question, I couldn't answer him.

I turned around and walked back to my seat staring at the embarrassed faces of my family. I couldn't explain, it was too complicated. I'd just gone down the rabbit hole.

CHAPTER 11

A Fish Called Tuna

Holiday ticket touts are armed with passes for every conceivable activity that you weren't planning. Armed with discounts for water parks to hair raising speed boats they will attempt to talk you into some kind of holiday adventure. From fishing for Marlin to mud baths in Dalyan, there's always a trip that takes you to dangerous waters. I've been on a sinking boat off the Gili islands, and I've also been onboard an airboat in waters full of alligators in the Everglades. During a trip to Lanzarote with all of our three children, we were talked into going onboard a replica pirate ship that certainly looked the part. From the main mast the skull and crossbones fluttered in the wind, while the crew dressed as pirates swung courageously high up on the rigging. Cannons fired as cheap drinks and chicken legs were brought up from the galley. Packed with families we headed away from the mainland into deeper waters. This was the mid-eighties and long before the days of the hit movie The Pirates of the Caribbean. The idea of being on a pirate cruise still captured the imagination of families and safety was not always on the organisers list of priorities. Funny how you can go on a huge cruise ship thousands of people onboard and go through the muster and lifeboat drill before you are allowed to leave port. Yet on a wooden ship with dozens of small children, fire torches and wine flowing for the adults, not a head count in sight. No discussions of emergency evacuations or a life jacket to be seen. I find this ironic considering you are always shown a life jacket on a plane. It seems that it is more important to know where your life jacket is in the sky but not on the water. As the entertainment caught everyone's attention, my nine-year-old son decided it was not that interesting. Perhaps he was more astute than the rest of us and viewed it as a poor representation. He insisted that I asked one of the crew if he could use the huge two handled fishing reel that was bolted to the railing at the back of the ship. The reel had a thick nylon line with a large hook secured to the rail. The hook was hidden and encapsulated inside a fake bright orange rubber squid. One of the crew members agreed to let my son drop the bait over the side and told him to let it trail some twenty yards behind us. Whispering into my ear, 'it's ok, he won't catch anything out here senor.' The frown had disappeared, and the ever-hopeful young fisherman was now holding on tightly with neither of us quite sure what a big rubber squid was supposed to attract. As time moved on the atmosphere of the ship became subdued as people sat quietly tucking into portions of salad, chicken and fries. Suddenly there was a loud series of clicks from the reel. It gave a sound like it was trying to lock into place. My son gave out a shout, something along the lines of 'got one,' and began turning the reel with all his strength. After a short time, it became apparent that whatever was on the end of the line needed an adult to haul it in. It took at least fifteen minutes to get the mystery catch to the stern of the boat. With a couple of more turns the bright orange squid broke through the surface of the waves. Hooked on to the squid was a tuna fish approximately three feet long. By now a crowd of onlookers had gathered around us and we were now very much the focal point. I had hauled the catch onto the deck and knew that I needed to remove the hook from the gaping mouth of this very lively fish. This tuna was not going to give up that easily and its smooth blue body felt dense and muscular. Having spent a lot of my youth fishing on the harbour entrance to the Isle of Man, I was quite familiar with the art of catching unhooking and gutting fish. I would take my catch to the back door of a Chinese restaurant in Strand Street and sell my catch of Grey Mullet and mackerel for a small fee.

Taking mullets and mackerel off a small hook was not difficult and as brutal as it sounds a quick bang on the head using the quay side bollards would be quick and acceptable. I was just about to tip this writhing brute back over the side when a member of the crew came up to me and said, 'great tuna, take it down below for the chef,' and then nonchalantly walked off. Shit, they want me to kill it. They seriously want me to kill it and give it to the cook below decks. I was now holding on to something that was fighting for its life, and I was hugging it like a small child. I inched over to the handrail that surrounded the ship and in a bending motion tried to bash its head on the rail. I looked like a Japanese black belt where they politely bow over and over before commencing to fight. Blood began to spray in all directions and this fish was eyeballing me as if to say, 'is that all you've got?' My tee shirt was spattered with red stains and smeared in fish scales. It looked like a scene from a chainsaw massacre, and I could hear the screams of terrified children behind me. For gods' sake die you bastard, I said under my breath. It seemed like the only thing gasping for breath was me and the only thing dying at this point was me, of sheer embarrassment. The fish was starting to get the crowd on side. It felt like I was nailing Jesus to the cross and his followers were totally appalled by my unflinching cruelty. When the mighty tuna finally succumbed to my inept mercy killing, I was completely exhausted. It would not have surprised me if some of the parents had thrown me overboard, considering the mental scars I'd now imprinted on to their children's holiday memories.

I carried the bloody fish down some stairs and presented it to the cook who was about the only person left on the boat who was pleased to see me. It was like Sweeney Todd greeting Jack the Ripper.

CHAPTER 12

The Pink Panther

As mentioned earlier in 'My Precious,' there is no better place to get scammed than on holiday.

It may be down to the fact that swindlers are well aware that people who are on vacation are relaxed and more likely to be off guard. We fall into a false sense of security due to the ambiance and the happy smiling faces that surround us. We allow ourselves to believe that nobody is trying to get a tip and they're always this friendly. Neither is anyone trying to get a tip because they gave you extra measures and complimented you on your amazing Hawaiian shirt. Everybody loves everybody at 'Sunny World,' even the cleaners. There are no thieves or criminals here and the police enjoy jovial banter with the tourists. They don't make arrests they make friends.

Our train from Rome to Venice had been a wonderful experience and the views from our carriage was amazing. Italian Cypress trees lined the hills of the countryside creating a beautiful backdrop to spectacular scenery. Old stone farmhouses sat like kings upon a throne at the top of gentle rolling hills. Every view that presented itself seemed to create portraits of Italy's amazing history. We passed through Florence, Bologna and Verona, and when we briefly stopped to pick up passengers i desperately wanted to get off and explore. After leaving Rome early on the Frecciarossa high speed train, we found ourselves in Venice less than three and a half hours later. Sadly Florence, Bologna and Verona would have to remain on the 'must see,' list. Venice was flooded! Did I really just say that? Venice was indeed underwater, not completely, but Saint Mark's Square was covered to a depth of twelve to eighteen inches. It never stopped raining from the moment we arrived at the Venezia Santa Lucia train station and it's fair to say, Venice loses a lot of its charm in shit weather. Thankfully our second day brought some lovely warm sunshine and by the mid-afternoon it had turned extremely hot. After browsing through the narrow lanes most of which were still flooded, we took a canal boat to the main promenade. We decided to take some lunch sitting outside a café called Circolo Sottufficiali which faced a small island by the name of San Giorgio Maggiore. Our two friends Andy and Shirley joined us, sharing two large pizzas and four large Stein beers. As the beer washed away the remnants of a thin crust Circolo special, my eyes suddenly caught the sight of a dishevelled gentleman crossing a small canal bridge maybe a hundred metres away from where we were sat. He was about five foot seven to five foot ten in height, but it was hard to tell as he was hunched over. His wavy hair was long and black, but it could not disguise his age which I estimated to be approximately late forties. Two striking features stood out even from a distance away. One, was the painful fact that this man had two club feet. To describe this more accurately, he was virtually walking on the outer edges of his shoes which meant only his little toe on each foot was touching the ground. Watching those twisted feet awkwardly hobble in my direction clutching a walking stick for support was bad enough but to see the man wearing a woman's three-quarter length pink coat was almost as painful. He took an age to negotiate the steps at the foot of the bridge and his walking stick now heralded his arrival onto to a smoother surface. Each harrowing step was matched by my guilt-ridden inability to swallow any more beer. My conscious battled with this awkward situation, and I sat watching intently with a stomach filled with overpriced pizza. In fact, it was so humbling that all other tables in our vicinity had fallen into a transfixed silence as they too stared despairingly at this man's plight. As he drew level with our table I stood up and walked past him dropping two euros into his plastic cup. I walked on past him towards the canal and peered towards the boats making their way back towards the St Marks landing point. I then turned about face and walked directly into the café toilets to relieve myself of at least half of the two pints I'd just consumed. As I re-joined my wife and friends back at the table I glanced in the direction of where I thought the guy in the pink coat would be heading for, but he had disappeared. As I sat down, I was greeted by raucous laughter and was asked how much money I'd donated to the man with the tortured feet? 'We know you dropped him some money,' they could hardly contain themselves. 'Where's he gone?' I asked, 'surely, he couldn't have got that far already?' Apparently while I was in the toilets the police had appeared in the distance and in the same direction to which the pink pretender was also heading. This prompted him to place his stick under his arm, straighten his feet and run like an Olympic athlete in the opposite direction. I was told that he cleared the steps onto the bridge by taking them all in one leap. My heart sank, once again I'd fallen for a scam, I wanted my money back. There is no greater plight than that of the homeless and it hurts me deeply. I've given money, drinks food and sat and talked with many homeless people about their situation. It's heart breaking and not always by choice. However, I've also witnessed the fraudulent gangs who operate in shifts and travel into cities on trains swapping locations and walking away using a mobile phone and changing into smarter clothing. I've watched as early morning fakes arrive and turn their jackets inside out to reveal a clever creation of dirty patch work. It's totally unfair on the genuine homeless and it's amazing how many people fall for it. Many people will do as I do and walk on by, but there are many people whose heart gets the better of them and toss over a pound or even more. In a prime location in a busy city centre a fair amount can be made by sitting on your arse. Take the case of Will Anderson, in 2015 he told a journalist from the new York post he made two hundred dollars an hour sitting with his dog Rizzo outside Grand Central station. The truth of the matter is that on holiday you are more likely to be scammed than you are at home.

CHAPTER 13

Viva Las Upgrade

The flight from Heathrow to Los Angeles was to be a connecting flight to get us to Las Vegas. We'd set off from Manchester and knew this was going to be a demanding trip. My son Adam had purchased a four-night stay for us at the Mirage hotel for our anniversary. We sat in comfortable seats at the front of the plane directly behind business class. Economy 'plus' seating offers a little more leg room for a few more dollars more. Three quarters of the way into the flight I started to notice the other passengers sat in the opposite isles. Some large black guys who looked like they could be American footballers were dressed in khaki shorts hoodies and sunglasses. I found this strange as it was a night flight, and the window covers were down, and the cabin was in low lighting. I became aware that at least twenty or perhaps thirty of these people all knew each other. A tall thin guy suddenly appeared from behind a curtain that separated us from the business class area. He looked to me a little bit like the football player Ronaldo, but with more hair. Before any fans of Bruno Mars start thinking I'm being disrespectful I also admit that while he was stood talking with his band members, he also reminded me a little bit of Michael Jackson. He asked his entourage if they were all okay and if they needed anything which made me realise that this chap was famous even if I didn't recognise him at the time. When we landed in LA my wife noticed the same crew of people pushing huge black and chrome edged boxes through the airport with the words 'Bruno Mars,' etched onto them in bold white letters. She decided to look up his name on Google and eventually said 'he's that famous pop singer, you know, I'd catch a grenade for you.' Mystery solved we moved on to our next flight which was a small jet plane with two seats on one side and one seat on the other. It was very much like a private jet, and it was not the first time I'd flown on such a small aircraft. I've flown on small planes from Manchester to Heathrow and from Georgia Atlanta to San Juan and if I'm honest, they scare the shit out of me. You feel the movement a lot more onboard smaller aircraft and for some peculiar reason you feel that you're traveling faster too, but you're not. We landed at McCarran airport, a place that welcomes the forty-one million tourists that visit Las Vegas every year. After picking up our luggage we joined the coach that was to take us to the Mirage hotel. As previously mentioned in an earlier chapter there's always going to be someone who is dropped off last and, on this occasion, it was us. It was great to get a tour of the city but after three flights and being on the go for twenty-four hours all we could think of was bed. The first thing that grabs you as you enter the Mirage hotel is the cacophony of noise. The fruit machines are clanging away mercilessly out of tune with each other. Spontaneous shouting and cheering comes from all directions and the lights are an epileptics nightmare. Behind the long reception desk was an equally long fish tank full of exotic multi coloured fish. We were greeted by a lady who was very polite yet robotic. She had done this speech a million times and could smile permanently while giving you all the instructions needed for your stay. We gratefully took our key card and headed towards the lifts. Floor six room fifty-two wasn't too difficult to find. The room itself was a basic design but also spotlessly clean and tidy. Although tired and exhausted from the hours of traveling we couldn't resist going out for a short walk. We had a brief look around the Mirage before crossing the street and taking a glimpse of the nightlife.

The Margaritaville bar was our first port of call, and it was packed tightly with party goers who were dancing the night away. It soon became apparent that the Las Vegas strip is not a place for jet lagged people with no idea of where they were going. We admitted defeat and wearily headed back to the hotel to catch up on some well-earned rest. The next day we met up with my daughter and son in law who'd flown in from Vancouver where they had both been living and working for the past twelve months. After the initial excitement of meeting up again, we set off for a walk, hoping to take in as many of the iconic sights that we could. It would be a long and tedious story if I started listing all the places that we'd managed to visit but if I had to name but a few I'd feel it's only right to mention the MGM. We unintentionally ended up at the weigh in for the fight between Manny Pacquiao versus Juan Manuel Marquez two of the world's greatest welterweights. My son in law Chris who follows the boxing quite closely, managed to get his photograph taken with Mike Tyson who commented on his T shirt bearing a picture of John Lennon. My daughter and son in law had now moved hotels and were staying at the Caesar's Palace. They had been staying somewhere off the strip and from what they'd told us, they may as well have been staying in a hostel. My wife thought it best to move them near to us and so they ended up in Caesar's Palace. Our room in the Mirage was great apart from the constant daylight. Even with curtains closed and the blinds shut it made no difference, the light penetrated the room and kept it a state of perpetual daylight. This artificial light was supplied by the floodlights that are positioned and angled outside the hotel to show it off in all its glory. The plan was to meet my daughter at eight o'clock at the Mirage restaurant and for us all to have a meal together. The plan however didn't go accordingly and while I was in the shower an accident occurred. The handle that controlled the shower was the biggest I'd ever seen. It was like the wheel you see on a submarine door when they lock them shut. I went to turn it off and it came away in my hand allowing jets of hot and cold water to spray uncontrollably into the bathroom. The hole in the wall was massive and I had to quickly hop out of the shower and leave the quickly flooding bathroom. In a panic I phoned reception and explained the dilemma.

Within minutes a maintenance guy knocked on the door and charged into the bathroom. He just stood there muttering and shaking his head, before talking into his walking talkie. 'Can't you stop it?' I asked him, standing there with just a towel around my waist. 'No can do, we got ourselves a fracture, just waiting on my buddy to get here. If you're heading out that's no problem, we'll have this sorted by time you get back.' Before I could explain that getting ready involved using the bathroom, his 'buddy' appeared through the door. A taller heavier man with a utility belt full of tools that looked too heavy to stay around his well-developed waistline. He walked straight past us without saying a word and straight into the bathroom. By now water was dripping from every wall and the floor was now one large puddle. He took out a lump hammer and chisel and started smashing away the tiles and bricks from where the shower lever once protruded. Shattered fragments of white ceramic tiles flew in every direction, even beyond the door and onto the floor where we were standing. 'I gotta do this so I can bend the pipe to stop the water, take me too long to turn it off at the main valve. Plus, it's gonna have to be rebuilt anyways.' I filmed the scene on my mobile as a backup knowing fine well that I had no choice but to complain. My daughter and son in law who'd been waiting for us, had now arrived at our room. In the meantime, I headed down to the reception armed with my film footage and started to devise my complaint speech. The receptionist asked me how he could help, and I started by showing him my film. I added that it was my anniversary tonight and by now we should have been sitting in the Mirage restaurant. I told him I couldn't get washed or shaved and we had no toilet as the water was about to be switched off. I then went full tilt by adding, my son had chosen and paid for this hotel believing it to be a well-known and highly reputable place. 'What's more my wife is so upset that our anniversary is turning into a disaster. What are you going to do about the room?' He looked at me nodding his head slowly on occasions to show he was being sympathetic with my situation. He then asked if he could borrow my phone while he went to speak to someone, which I presumed would be his manager. Sure enough, another man appeared a little older and dressed smartly in a distinctive black uniform. He handed back my phone and at the same time calmly asked me for my key card. 'You won't be needing this,' he said, casually throwing it over his shoulder. 'I'd like to apologise on behalf of the Mirage hotel and please let me resolve this situation in the best way that I can.' He started to type on a keyboard somewhere below the desk and out of sight. He then produced a new key card and slowly began to explain what he'd done. 'As you are going to be late for your special meal, I have put two hundred dollars on this card to be spent in any of the restaurants in the Mirage. I have moved you to a suite on the top floor of the hotel that has your own private lift.' This seemed a fair amount of compensation and i happily accepted. Perhaps i could have pushed it for something more but how often do you get offered a suite in las Vegas? I returned to our original room and explained what had happened at the reception and we quickly gathered our things together and headed to our new room. The suite was incredible and being on the top floor it had an amazing view of Vegas and the famous strip. We were enthralled by the big television which came out of the base of the bed and the bathroom had a television on the wall. There was a walk-in wardrobe that was bigger than some of the hotel rooms I've stayed in previously and the living room had a full-sized bar in the corner. Half an hour later the novelty had worn off and we made our way down to the restaurant. After a great evening which again included taking in as many sights as possible, we stumbled exhausted into our private lift. The lift although ordained as private is not strictly for those guests on the top floor suites. Anyone staying in any of the top three floors could use the lift. I must admit I enjoyed the brief glances when people dressed in their finery had to exit the lift before we did. The same looks from the same type of people when my wife and I sat at the captain's table on the Norwegian Spirit. Truth is, a holiday shouldn't be about the room where you're staying, or the food that you eat or even the service. It's about the whole experience and more importantly new experiences. I've stayed in beautiful spacious villas, and I've also stayed in a bungalow in the jungle with an outside toilet, I remember them both with equal fondness.

CHAPTER 14

That Sinking Feeling

The Lombok straights runs between the coast of Bali and the coast of Lombok and has a reputation of being a very rough passage. This is due to the tidal mix between the Indian Ocean and the Pacific Ocean. Without getting into marine technicalities the deep waters and currents around these areas create a turbulent merging of some bloody big waves. Six of us had met up at a hotel in Seminyak, which included my sister and brother-in-law and my son and his friend, all from Perth Australia. It was to be a round trip of a few islands off Bali and our first port of call was to an island called Nusa Lembongan. Its a large island which is about an hour's journey by fast boat and surprisingly doesn't have a landing stage. As we were effectively on a water taxi that holds around a hundred people we were surprised when we suddenly stopped engines and just floated at the entrance to a wide estuary. Minutes later we were asked to climb down to a small fishing type boat that just about fitted the six of us and our luggage. The smaller boat is used to get people up the shallow estuary to what is known locally as the 'famous yellow bridge.' The smaller boat that we'd climbed into stopped fifteen minutes later at an inlet that was still twenty yards from the shore. The distant shoreline consisted of a line of mango trees with countless twisting roots spearing into the banks of the muddy waters. We were told that this was as far as the pilot of our boat could take us. Climbing over the edge of the small boat and lowering ourselves into the water felt surreal. The water was warm and came up to my chest and just up to my wife's shoulders. A human chain from the tallest to shortest naturally formed a line from boat to shore and we passed the suitcases to each other by lifting them above our heads. This wasn't expected but is sure gave us a feeling of adventure. My apologies to mountain climbers, bungie jumpers, surfers and sky divers. Adventure comes at whatever level you can handle. Surfers are always looking for that bigger and better wave to ride, while others are quite content with a pedalo. Staying on a nautical theme, it was during our stay in Lembongan that we took a small boat to a place called Manta point, off the nearby island of Nusa Penida. Famous for allowing people to swim alongside groups of giant manta rays, I guess it's how they decided on its name. A small Balinese fishing boat transported us to a rocky cove, and we snorkelled for an hour or so alongside these elegant sea-creatures. You suddenly feel like Jacque Cousteau, or for any younger readers let's make that Aqua man. Swimming with these amazing relatives of the shark family is an unforgettable experience. That is except for one man who went on the same trip shortly after we had in 2017. Travelling to the same spot, retired postman Alan Pope survived a miraculous if not terrifying incident. A swordfish launched itself out of the sea and straight through Mr Popes neck. Missing his jugular vein by millimetres the fish snapped away from its beak and somehow flipped back into the ocean, leaving Mr Pope in a precarious life-threatening situation.

On our trip we had battled some high waves to get to Manta ray point, during which time my sister-in-law had called out nervously that we were all going to die. Mr Pope and his wife, however, must have thought that death was inevitable, given what must have been an incredibly long boat journey back to Nusa Lembongan and then onto Bali.

Mr Pope survived after some precarious surgery lasting over three and a half hours. Surgeons managed to remove the foreign body from his neck and as a reminder he now sports a tattoo of a sword fish on his arm. At this moment I'd like to bring back the fear of flying and how it affects us mentally. Let's imagine

Mr Pope was also terrified of flying and his wife had said, 'but darling there's more chance of you being hit in the neck by a swordfish.' Need i say more?

A few days later we boarded the fast boat to the Gili islands which is a group of small islands north of Lombok. The Gili islands consists of three very small Islands named, Air, Meno, and Trawangan. Surrounded by palm trees and white beaches it must be one of the most beautiful places on earth. The only form of transport on the islands are small horse drawn carriages that tightly fit four people plus their luggage on board. The warm water around the islands holds an abundance of sea life that dazzles you with a variety of vibrant colours. Clown fish and Butterfly fish swim effortlessly between the sculptured coral branches, designed by millions of minute polyps. There are many restaurants serving sumptuous food including freshly caught fish such as red snapper and other traditional Balinese fare. But as the saying nearly goes, the grass is possibly greener on the other island, which meant we needed to catch a boat over to Trawangan to find out why it was the most popular of the three islands. Trawangan was a far livelier than Gili Air and does have a reputation as a party island. It was early afternoon when we arrived, and the atmosphere was a little subdued, so we decided to take a walk around the outskirts. The island was going through a transitional phase due to a law that had been passed recently to remove all bars and restaurants from off the beach and back onto dry land. This was leaving behind some ugly foundations and iron work which were not in keeping with the idyllic otherwise beautiful scenery. Considering there are no police on the islands the laws that existed were being followed to the letter. When it came to dealing with any petty law breakers it was often the village chief who decided the punishment of anyone who crossed the line. It has been well documented that when two Australian women stole a bike from outside one of the hotels their punishment was to walk around the island with signs hanging around their necks saying, 'I am a thief.' The only signs that concerned us on our visit to Trawangan, were the signs of bad weather approaching. The light began to fade quickly and the haste of people leaving the beach signalled that the distant black clouds were heading our way. The wind caught everybody by surprise as it charged down the main thoroughfare causing the ponies to become agitated as they sensed the ominous changes in the air. We knew it was time to leave and head back to our own island and started to walk towards the main pier for boat transfers. We had arrived on the boat that had brought people from the mainland and drops and collects at each island. The wind was beginning to gust through the smaller streets, and you could feel an uneasy presence amongst the local traders as they scurried to put their items into secure areas. My son had suggested we get back to Gili Air as quickly as possible concerned that the main boats may refuse to run if the weather gets any worse and we may find ourselves stranded. In hindsight being stranded on Gili Trawangan was probably the better outcome. Rather than wait for the main boat to arrive my son had negotiated a fee with two young fishermen to take us back to Gili Air on their small fishing boat. It looked seaworthy enough, but I felt apprehensive as the eldest looked no older than sixteen and the younger around thirteen. Not exactly old sea dogs with years of experience behind them. The first sign that this trip was doomed to failure was when they tried to start the engine and realised, they needed more petrol. The youngest boy dashed off and returned in less than a minute with more fuel inside a plastic bottle. The older boy poured the extra petrol into the top of the engine and began pulling the starter chord to fire up the engine. The younger boy pushed us away from the shore and jumped back in to join whom I thought must be his friend or brother. The initial distance travelled out into the bay was slightly bumpy but nothing out of the ordinary. As we reached open water the waves got progressively worse, lapping at the side of the boat as if desperately trying to climb aboard. Heading into the wind, the route was to take us around the northern tip of the island of Gili Meno which was located between Trawangan and Gili Air. The two boys who were huddled together at the back of the boat, were taken by surprise when the familiar noise of the engine suddenly cut out. An eerie silence caused us to stare awkwardly at the older boy who was desperately trying to restart the engine. As he pulled at the chord, parts of the engine housing started to fall away. It was now that I noticed that pieces of string had been holding this engine together. My heart sank as I watched the boy fall from side to side, struggling to keep his balance while trying to piece back together the components that would keep us moving. I watched with some guilt at his predicament, feeling that he should never have accepted our offer. A plume of grey smoke signalled that the engine was back in action, and we continued into the headwind. The bottom of the boat had acquired a swirling pool of water that was sloshing from side to side and rolling between our feet. More water spilled into the boat from the oncoming waves that were now crashing over the bow. As the wind became stronger so too did the waves and the nervous laughter that had greeted the situation had long since expired. The boat was becoming perilously close to capsizing as it rolled uncontrollably each time another wave hit us side on. We stared at each other, no smiles, just long stares to say, 'are you thinking what I'm thinking?' My son's friend had seen enough, and she shouted nervously at the young boys to put us off as close to the shore as they could. I think by now we had accepted that we may have to swim for land depending on how close they could get us to the coastline of Gili Meno. Without question or hesitation, the older boy turned the boat to face the shoreline and tried to manoeuvre his vessel towards a safe landing area. The waves pushed the boat back out towards the open water, and we knew that it was an impossible task to get us anywhere near to shallow waters. Taking hold of our bags, we each jumped into the sea one by one and scrambled our way to the shoreline. It was deep enough to swim but also shallow enough to stand. Here's a handy tip, get yourself one of those thick waterproof dry bags, marvellous on a beach holiday and very handy if you're on a sinking boat. By the time we dragged ourselves onto some rough ground the two boys and the boat had disappeared. It had either sunk or was now heading home at great speed with the wind and the waves in their favour. With the island being so small it wasn't long before we came across a path that would lead us to shelter. People sitting at a remote hotel bar where quite shocked to see us walking towards them soaked and dishevelled. They must have wondered why four people had arrived soaked to the skin from a remote area and soon our story was known to all. We were given some towels to help dry off and some coffee to warm us up. In my early thirties I had passed an offshore course which involved escaping from a helicopter that turns upside down while under water, I was terrified at the time. I was more terrified of being thrown into the sea miles from land and knew that the outcome of our trip could have been far worse.

They say lightening never strikes twice in the same spot. That may be so, but there are records of people being hit by lightning on more than one occasion. Roy Sullivan who lived in Virginia USA, has been hit seven times and has his place in the Guinness Book of records. When the time came for us to leave the Gili islands we boarded the 'fast boat' to return to Bali. The Ekajaya arrived an hour later than expected and by the time everybody's luggage was loaded, it was five o'clock in the evening. The interior of the boat is filled with comfortable seats that span the width and the entire length of the boat. Similar to an aeroplane, except it has five seats either side. In good weather it's possible to sit on the roof top and get a superb view of the surrounding coastline. An hour into the journey it was noticeable that the weather was beginning to change quickly, and the boat was lifting and dropping with a loud thumping sound on the underside of the hull. All the passengers onboard had been told that they were to be seated inside the boat and were no longer permitted to go outside. The daylight had now disappeared and the only part of the outside world that was visible was the waves rolling past the windows. This gave the illusion of being underwater or trapped inside a washing machine. It got progressively worse, and as the waves began to build so did the fear onboard. The Lombok straights has a reputation for horrendous sea conditions and a quick search on Trip Advisor will give you a good insight into its history. Treacherous four-metre-high waves are not uncommon and just to add to the sense of foreboding, there is no Air Sea Rescue or lifeboats operating here, as you would expect in the UK. As we tried desperately to concentrate on the movie that was being played on the two large televisions, the lights above us started to flicker. The Transformers movie had helped as a distraction from what was ultimately a real-life Poseidon adventure. Thinking that at any moment the boat was going to overturn was becoming a regular occurrence for me. The lights continued to flicker incessantly and then just to add to our mental torture they cut out. Along with both televisions and any other electrical lighting we were plunged into darkness. But that wasn't the worst of it. The engines had stopped, and their constant humming was no longer audible. In no time at all we had stopped dead in the ocean. Fighting your way through the snarling waves with engine power is hard enough, but with nothing to push you forward, it's a dam sight worse. We rolled from side to side and all that could be heard was the wind and the waves smashing against the sides of the boat. To make things worse the sound of a baby crying and screaming loudly and every so often someone would vomit uncontrollably. Although the engines weren't running the smell of diesel wafted around the cabin adding to the nauseating atmosphere. The air conditioning had also lost its power and the heat and humidity mixed with diesel and the stench of vomit took the claustrophobic room to an unbearable level. Four young Irish lads who'd been entertaining us with tales of their recent climbing expedition were now all sat with their heads in their hands. They had recently climbed to the top of mount Rinjani, the second highest volcano in all of Indonesia. Four days of camping in swirling mist and clouds meant that they didn't get to see anything, when arriving at its summit. One of the lads was becoming nervous and agitated and I'm sure the rest of us where not far off. The crew who was probably thoroughly used to these conditions gave little empathy to its sick passengers. The Irish lads were now starting to be sick in unison and it wasn't long before the whole boat caught a whiff of the dreaded odour. Like yawning the disgusting stench only served to promote and prompt others to reach for their sick bags. Half an hour past by and we anxiously waited for one of the crew to give us some news. Apart from the odd attempt to restart the engines we remained static and in almost complete darkness. Some emergency lighting did help lift our spirits but with regards to future prospects no information was forthcoming. Perhaps many of us believed that another boat had been radioed to come to our assistance or even to tow us home. Then without warning the televisions and lights lit up the cabin. The unmistakable sound of the engines firing back up were greeted with a cheer. The boat surged forward slowly at first and then with an almighty roar picked up speed very quickly.

This was such a welcome relief as it instantly helped stabilise the boat. The journey to Bali still involved being hammered by mountainous waves but under the circumstances they were far more acceptable.

The lights of Padangbai harbour where welcome a sight as you could wish for, and we were overjoyed to step off the boat and onto its wooden pier. If the journey didn't kill you the pier certainly could. As we stood huddled together waiting for our rucksacks to be unloaded, we could hear the shouts of local people shouting, careful, must be careful,' while pointing to the timber decking beneath our feet. The pier had seen better days and there was evidence of a new pier yards away under construction. This current pier was a death trap with huge holes randomly appearing across its whole platform. One small lapse of concentration and you would fall to the rocks down below. Bali is the only place where the police get on the boat to do a head count to make sure it's not overloaded but at the same time allow the pier where you get on and off to be a death trap. If you've ever watched 'Squid Game,' you'll get a feeling for how the 'collect your luggage,' game goes.

CHAPTER 15

Is There Another Doctor Onboard?

The eagerly awaited introduction of Boeing's Dreamliner aircraft was making news all over the world. This was to be a plane built to incorporate new designs and materials in order to change the concept of flying. With the new advances in technology the engines and structure of the Dreamliner were ground-breaking. Possibly not the best turn of phrase for something that flies. Even the lower mortals in cattle class were getting some added refinement. Windows had been installed that were bigger and dimmable to stop glare from ruining the view of the horizon. Better air quality filtered from the outside of the aircraft. Mood lighting to provide an ambience to match the time of day, blue to help keep you awake and lively, with a dusky pink during evening and night flights. Regardless of the advances in technology our Dreamliner departed Grantley Adams airport one hour late. Barbados to the UK should have taken approximately eight hours thirty minutes depending on the weather, tail winds, air pressure and host of other conditions. Our friends of over twenty years had kindly joined us on our Caribbean cruise to see us renew our vows. Sitting together we were lucky enough to have been given the extra leg room seats which where adjacent to the aircraft door near the front of the plane. Our friend who was sat nearest to the window first noticed an incessant dripping of water just after taking off. As we finished climbing and levelled out, the water from above her head had turned from a drip into trickle, which was now hitting her directly on her head. I found this quite

CLOSE ENCOUNTERS OF THE HOLIDAY KIND

amusing, mostly because she didn't. She pressed the call button for a cabin crew member to take a look at the impromptu waterfall and to see if it could be plugged. After a brief assessment the crew member duly apologised and stuffed a blanket in the top box above my friend's head. It did the trick and the leak stopped but it does beg the question, where was it coming from? You then think, electrics, water, thirty-five thousand feet, surely a recipe for disaster. Six hours later, no turbulence, no water, no problems, just your average straight forward flight. But that was all to change as the pilot called out, 'is there a doctor onboard and if so, can you make yourself known to the cabin crew?' There are code words used on flights by pilots and the crew, which are used not to raise alarm amongst the passengers. Examples would be, '7500,' which means there's a possible hijack taking place, or 'code Adam,' meaning a child has gone missing.' A' Deadhead,' is a fellow steward being transported on the plane as a passenger to join another aircraft. The worst must be 'crop dusting,' if a crew member mentions this to one of their own it means they have a rude customer and they are going to stand arse to passenger face and fart. Childish revenge and you just wouldn't think those glamorous people were capable, would you? The captain asking for a doctor, is not a coded phrase to disguise some impending disaster that may or may not happen. It's an outright plea to save the life of someone who's going to end up stiffer than the rest of us in the cheap seats. I find it amazing that the two times I've heard a call for a doctor onboard a flight, that there has indeed been a doctor on both of those flights. This begs the question, what would happen if there wasn't a doctor onboard. Does the captain work his way down a list of 'next best?' 'Is there a paramedic onboard? No, okay, is there a vet onboard? No, erm, is there anyone out there who played the game 'Operation,' and managed to take out the funny bone without making the red nose buzzer go off?' The crew would no doubt scrutinise the passenger list and if they don't see the abbreviation 'Dr,' on the list, they must get the pilot to call out. So, there you have it one more reason why taking to the skies is a risky business unless your married to a surgeon and you're on the same trip. As luck would have it there was a Doctor on this flight, and he pressed his call button to make himself known. I watched as the crew spoke to him and then quickly led him to the rear of the plane. The fasten your seat belt sign was on to allow better movement around the isle of the plane and for the captain to go and meet the doctor. The flight continued as you'd expect until another announcement came from the captain. 'Good evening, ladies and gentlemen, as you may have noticed we have a person onboard who has unfortunately been taken seriously ill. We have received advice from our headquarters and the aviation authority that we need to seek medical attention for our passenger as soon as possible. Given our current position we will now be making an emergency landing in the Azores. I will do my best to keep you all updated and will let you know if there are any other changes. Thank you for your understanding.' Thirty minutes later we had landed at a military base on the island of Terceira. The Azores are an archipelago based in the mid-Atlantic and an autonomous region of Portugal. The captain came to the PA system and stood in front of the passengers to make his next announcement. 'Ladies and gentlemen, we have landed at this airport to get our passenger the urgent medical attention he needs. Please don't be alarmed, but you will see some paramedics and a medical team boarding the plane. Outside you will see some flashing lights from the emergency vehicles, again there is no cause for concern.' It took over an hour before the passenger in question was wheeled down the aisle to be lifted from the plane. It came to light that the passenger who'd taken ill had been to Central Africa before heading to Barbados which had coincided with a recent case of Ebola in the African city he had visited. A short time later we were told that the passenger was cleared of any health conditions that were subject to quarantine. It was now time for the captain to make a third and final announcement. 'Ladies and gentlemen, unfortunately due to the time that has now elapsed,

I now don't have enough flying hours left to get us back to the U.K. Coaches are being arranged to take you to a hotel where you will stay overnight and will return tomorrow afternoon. Due to security risks, you will not be able to collect your luggage and all cases will remain on the aircraft. If I could fly you home, I'd be more than happy to do so, but the rules regarding flying hours are very strict.' Well fuck me, wasn't the man with the heart attack suddenly the most unpopular man on the plane. Sympathy, evaporated and turned into condemnation. 'He shouldn't have got on the plane if he was feeling ill, dickhead. Selfish bastard, what if he did have Ebola, we'd all be lying next to him in the same fucking ward.' We're like that us Brits, we sympathise then criticise if it impacts on our own well-being.

The Azores coaches took us over some rolling hills to a town twelve miles away called Angra Do Herismo. We pulled up outside a smart but ageing hotel called the 'Ilha,' and a guide led us into the reception area to book us all in. This hotel had been closed for winter until our arrival and some staff had been contacted to help make up the beds and offer us some refreshments. We were served a bowl of tinned fruit cocktail and a coffee and that was it. After pigging out on a cruise for ten days, this was, I am ashamed to say, devastating. It was January 2015 and it looked like the town had gone into hibernation. We walked for miles and the only people we came across were other passengers off the plane. It was like an episode of lost. Close to cannibalism we were delighted to find a small Chinese owned grocery shop which was still open and managed to stave off our hunger with a couple of chicken and mushroom pot noodles. The following morning, we still had enough time to explore the town and take in the sights. There seemed to be historical churches on every street and brightly painted buildings around every corner. The roads and pavements were created with black and white cobblestones that shone in the cold morning sunlight. Their appearance resembled an old Roman mosaic far too elegant for a simple pedestrian path. The harbour was full of sleepy boats tilted to one side resting on a golden Sandy beach. It's hard to believe that the Azores are not mentioned as a holiday destination in the same way as perhaps the Canary Islands. Perhaps their location doesn't offer the same all year round temperatures, but they certainly boasted some great scenery. By mid-afternoon we were back on our plane and setting off for home. For all the travel hints you could possibly read, I don't think taking a pair of spare underpants in your pocket gets a mention but there is a good argument. Mrs Hinch's handy hints have become hugely popular over recent years and it seems that bicarbonate of soda cleans everything. So, with that in mind, the next chapter of this book is going to be a collection of the most valuable travel tips that I can recommend.

CHAPTER 16

Don't Put All Your Eggs In One Omelette

Arrive at the airport with naked except for your underpants or a pair of trunks. This will ensure a very quick transition through security. A Bikini would also narrow down any searches or questions relating to any dangerous items on your person?

Don't smile at anyone, it looks like your trying to hide something or your showing off because you've just had your teeth whitened.

Don't think smiling at everyone will make airport staff think you're a nice person and not consider you to be a threat. They will do the opposite and probably drug test you. Nobody should be smiling in an airport queue.

Don't ever answer a security question with the Jim Royle catch phrase, 'my arse,' especially when asked 'are you carrying any illegal substances?'

Don't flush the airplane toilet whilst seated. The suction is equal to a black hole. Baboons are used to test these appliances when fitted. Do i need to say more?

Don't start a drunken brawl on a flight, especially over Thailand. The Bangkok Hilton is not a hotel. Many other countries offer similar accommodation to criminals and in certain justice systems your court case will be heard directly after the Count of Monte Christo's.

Never ever joke about bombs on planes, it's not funny and it's never going to get the reaction you may think. I was going on a cycling holiday in Lanzarote and the security team found a fairly expensive bicycle pump in my carry-on bag. They took it off me and to be honest i was a bit peed off. I was just about to say, 'I'm not going to 'blow up' as in 'inflate,' the plane,' get it? Then suddenly thought better of it. A passenger on a flight from Warsaw to Egypt in 2015 made a joke about a bomb being onboard and caused the plane to be diverted to Bulgaria where he was arrested and detained. Little is known of the outcome, but it does carry a 15 year sentence in Bulgaria. How many famous people can you name from Bulgaria? Exactly, no one gets out of this country. They live right next to the Black Sea, not the Golden Ocean or the Sea of serenity. They have towns called Tartarla and Suloglu, which sound to me like a scousers good bye and something sticky.

People swear by rolling up your clothing you can fit more into a suitcase and its stops it from wrinkling. This is not true, you will still end up ironing it. The only think that this technique works for is socks.

CHAPTER 17

Where the Odd Socks Go

Scientists are always working on complex theories that have little or no meaning to most of us. The Halogen Collider spends the day bashing atoms together, that much i do know. Why scientist are doing this, i have no idea? The study of 'Black Holes, will tell us what exactly? String theory, Quantum theory, Big Bang theory, i wonder what purpose they will serve. How come these scientific super egg heads don't work on the 'Odd Sock Theory?' In my lifetime I must have lost a thousand socks therefore putting the other thousand socks into the black hole, otherwise known as the rubbish bin. I don't lose my mobile phone and I take it everywhere. Nor do I lose my car keys as that would be a spectacular fail. So, this makes me wonder how I manage to lose one sock that can only be in one of three places. In my sock drawer, on my foot, or in the washing machine. Taking the 'on my foot,' out of the equation, let's face it, you can't lose it when it's actually on your foot, this leaves the other two locations. But the other two places are in the house, therefore it leaves little scope for proving the point where they disappeared too. I think if they manage to send a probe into a black hole one day, they will find a huge woollen ball made entirely of socks. To be fair, socks are small and insignificant, especially when you compare them to a great big fat heavy suitcase. Notice the way i emphasize on dimensions here? And by now you've probably twigged where I'm going with this, the 'lost luggage, 'theory. In the top ten of holiday disasters this is well and truly up there. Perhaps breaking a limb on the water slide or the cord snapping on a bungee jump is possibly worse, but not meeting up with your luggage at your arrival airport is an absolute disaster. To lose your suitcase on your way home isn't great but you can at least compensate for the lost items once you walk through your front door. Standing at an airport carousel watching an empty black belt rattle around in circles without any other passengers for company is only the beginning of your lonely trip to hell. It's happened to me a few times and it can rip your emotions to the point of despair. Let's do what the clever scientists do and start with a hypothesis. You arrived at the airport, and you definitely still had your cases with you when you weighed them in, obviously. Ok, good start. The suitcases had the worlds stickiest destination tickets around their handles, surely that's a good thing. They went on the same conveyor belt as all the other passengers luggage on your flight, another good point. But now they're lost and your standing in Bali airport wondering why the person who sat next to you on the same flight has managed to easily pluck theirs off the conveyer belt like the star prize on 'Wheel of Fortune.'

First of all, we must highlight the consequences this brings. You will eventually be told to go to your onward destination and wait while the airline tries to locate your luggage. You will sit in your hotel room without a change of underwear or toothbrush. Then it hits home, your shaver, new shoes, new clothes and expensive perfumes are also at the mercy of lost property. Then you remember that tomorrow you will be catching a boat to a remote island for the remainder of your holiday. Now for some good news, on the occasions that this has happened to me, I have been reunited with my luggage quite quickly. In Bali I was given my luggage at four am in the morning by our hotel porter. I told him to knock the minute it arrived. Possibly not the best decision I've ever made but I was so happy to see our luggage, I welcomed my rucksack like a long lost relative, hugging and kissing it. On another occasion our luggage was given to us three days after we had arrived back home, having flown from Atlanta Georgia to Manchester. So, the moral of the story is don't put all your eggs in one basket. Split your belongings across suitcases if you're travelling with more than one person. Therefore, a fifty fifty chance that at least one piece of luggage arrives at your destination. Once your luggage disappears behind the smiling airport check in rep, it goes into the equivalent of monsters inc where there's a thousand doors it can go through next. There are some sure signs that you won't be seeing your luggage on the other side and even a 'Spiritualist,' won't help you contact your dearly departed Samsonite. The first tell-tale sign is having to dash for a connecting flight. If, your first flight landed behind schedule and you end up racing across terminals to get to your next flight, you can bet your suitcases are still on the first flight. With any luck they will get put on the next flight and you will be reunited sometime later. Another similar scenario, is if you miss your connecting flight, and you are told you can go and queue at another flight desk with a later flight back to the UK. If you're lucky and the flight isn't full, they'll call you up. If like me you do get a spare seat on a flight, then you will come to realise that there is no way that Sully and Mike down in the bowels of terminal three know what flight you're getting on. It's enough to make you scream and enough to question why you take a suitcase in the first place? This is something my wife and I have learnt to live without recently on smaller journeys. We found that being practical and doing a little washing while away, means you can reduce your clothing requirements significantly. Most of us take too many clothes to begin with and it's amazing how often you don't need certain items when you get to where you're going. Many places we visit often sell clothes much cheaper than the similar items we buy at home. Suitcases will inevitability go missing, meaning people are now tying bits of bright cloth or putting stickers on their luggage to make them instantly recognisable. Perhaps we should all get suitcases with a picture of our faces laser printed on to them. Maybe not a great idea for some politicians or celebrities as they may never see their luggage again. Imagine being a baggage handler and seeing Piers Morgan or Boris Johnston's mush sliding down the gantry. And of course, this approach wouldn't have been great for the likes of Pablo Escobar. Recently the airlines have caught on to how savvy we're all getting and now charge for cabin baggage. This has developed into a constant battle between them and us and how they keep thinking of new methods of extracting more money from us. We in return keep looking at how we can find a way around their excessive day light robbery. Strange how everybody turned up at the airport without pre booking their seats and still sat next to each other. Now we pay for the privilege of sitting next to each other. If another passenger asks if ill swap seats so they can be near their friend or family member should i charge them?

They used to mark a suitcase case as 'heavy,' now they charge you huge amounts for every kilo over the given allowance. Passengers then hold up the queue trying to move items from one case to another. Some even resort to putting on extra clothes from out of the suitcase. Ridiculous when you think about it, because the plane will still be carrying the same weight. There's also the 'if it doesn't fit in this box,' you can't take it on board. A metal square container that your onboard luggage must fit into before boarding. The solution to all these weights and measures is easy. At the front of the check in desk they should have a set of scales that you also step onto alongside your luggage. Then you would scan your passport which tells the scales, 'sixty year old man,' 'height five foot eleven.' Body weight should be X with plus and minus five kilograms allowance. Plus, twenty two kilos, for baggage. Total up and there you go a 'a fat bastard tax,' can now be implemented. If I'm overweight for my age and height according to my digital passport I get hit with an excessive skin baggage tax or we could call it something like 'Transporkage tax.' Imagine the health benefits worldwide. There's going to be programs on television called, Get Ready for Take Off,' holiday exercises with Judith Chalmers. Imagine everyone standing around the pool looking gymtastic, no big queues at the buffet and not a plastic pint of beer in sight. The fear of stepping on those scales on your return flight will stop anyone gorging on pizza and chips. 'Welcome Senor Gallagher, I see you ad, ow you say a gooooood olly day, si? 'The ears of the queue all prick up behind me as the airport check in guy announces that I have fallen into Porkage duty Passenger' range, and I will need to pay the extra seating tax for the wider seats on the back of the plane. Due to the new healthier slimmer passengers were now seeing, 'Tightarse Airlines.com' can now introduce rows of four seats either side of the plane with a seat dimension of super model. Nobody eats or drinks wine on the plane anymore as the inflight dining options on offer are now Slim-shakes and crab sticks. The Hen parties and Stag do's have decided that it's cheaper to kick the shit out of each other by staying at home and we no longer have any impromptu fighting onboard the plane from pissed up passengers. No longer do I have to witness the younger generations taking selfies at seven o'clock in the morning over a full English breakfast wearing sunglasses and pouting like they just had the air sucked out of their body like one of those vacuum seal bags. I can't imagine what they write on Face book, 'yeh having a maze time, just got fried eggs and beans with sausage at 'Giraffe,' restaurant Manchester airport, living the dream.'

CHAPTER 18

When in Rome

One city that has to be on every traveller's list should be Rome. The eternal city is a modern day time machine with the ability to transport its visitors to some of the greatest moments in history. Built around 753 BC it claimed to be the capital of the world and on inspection it's hard to disagree. Where else would you find another country that sits inside a city? The Vatican has a status that is world renowned and as previously mentioned has its own separate history which is full of scandal, blood and gore. That honour you would think is normally reserved for the Colosseum, but you'd be wrong. During the 1400's the Borgias created a dynasty that thrived on building a cruel and corrupt society. Twisting religious values to safeguard its wealthy inheritance, it knowingly spilt blood for a very different cause. Pope Alexander IV was rumoured to have more than two illegitimate children and it seems that he spent most of his days running something close to a modern day mafia. Roll forward to summer 2017 and our arrival at Fiumicino airport was greeted with blue skies and warm sunshine. Along with our two friends, my wife and I were just adding to the other nine million estimated visitors that arrived in Rome each year. Our hotel was a small building and located on the outskirts the city. A clean place and a good base for exploring the city, we certainly had no intention of lounging about the swimming pool. I was truly excited at the thought of standing in the Colosseum and as soon as we had checked in, we set off for the city. The weather had been a mixture of sunshine and rain before we had arrived, but the forecast said it was going to be sunny and hot over the next couple of days. True to its word the forecast brought some glorious sunshine which seemed to add to the magnitude of the historical structures that surrounded us. Secretly my heart was pounding as we walked up to the entrance to the colosseum. It was a little smaller than I'd imagined, but at the same time it must have been hugely intimidating when completed in 79 AD. Although we see it as a world famous landmark today, many people through history would have seen it as a death sentence. When the Roman emperor Titus declared one hundred days of games, there were over five thousand people killed within its walls. It is estimated that four hundred thousand gladiators died in the colosseum, along with criminals, animals and even women. Today it's left to your imagination along with some descriptive plaques to help visualise the violence and ferocity that took place exactly beneath your feet. The crumbling ruins only give a partial feeling to the once glittering festivities. You can't help but see Russel Crowe, Charlton Heston and Kirk Douglas, fighting for their Hollywood wages and suddenly hear the shout of 'I'm Spartacus,' somewhere in the back of your mind. A wasp flying around my face brought me back to reality and it became a nuisance as it weirdly kept bumbling into my forehead. I started swinging wildly at it catching some smiles from those people in the vicinity. Finally stomping my size tens triumphantly down on its black and yellow armour, I realised that I had now joined the ranks of Maximus Decimus Meridius. From high up in the galleries you can see the arch of Constantine which welcomed any returning hero's back to the city of Rome. From here the walk along the ancient Roman road of Via Sacra begins and leads up to the Senatorial Palace. From the roof top of the palace, it is easy to see why Rome is unequalled for its famous historical sites. At the same time, one can also appreciate that it is still an eternal city, with a modern day thriving culture. For us the day had been long and arduous having marched from one famous site to another. The Trevi fountains are not within easy walking distance from the Colosseum and the Vatican City is a good hike from any other major location. Absolutely shattered and ready to relax we took a train from a central city station which was supposed to take us to the Appiano train station a four minute walk from our hotel. The Grand hotel Tiberio was about thirty minutes away and as we boarded the train, we had no choice but to stand near the doors as all the seats were taken. It was rush hour and people were heading home from work and every carriage was packed solid. After about fifteen minutes we made our first stop and I recognised the station, it was the place we'd changed trains on our way in. Strange that we were not changing trains on the way back I thought. Without speaking to each other it was noticeable how we seemed to be hurtling straight through other stations without stopping. Since leaving the last station we were now travelling at an exceptional speed. The tightly packed buildings and houses were beginning to thin out and give way to fields and countryside. The prolific graffiti that seemed to adorn every building that run alongside the railway tracks had disappeared altogether. For us however the writing was on the wall, we'd only gone and caught an express train to the suburbs. After managing to find a very helpful gentleman who thankfully spoke good English, we understood that the next stop was some fifteen minutes away and we would need to get off. We were heading for the port of Civitavecchia that only included stops at major towns along the way. When we did stop at the next station, the man who obviously knew he had time to spare, guided us to the platform that would get us back to Rome. It was a longer trip back but when we finally arrived at our hotel, we wasted no time in getting ourselves back out, to grab some food at a local restaurant. The restaurant was a small establishment and i sadly cannot recall its name. Serving us with an authentic Italian meal and a little slice of Italian hospitality it was not much bigger than the houses in the street. After our meal we strolled along few streets before stopping at a bar called 'Ultra Bar,' Just off the Piazza Giovanale. Adorned with football memorabilia including an Everton scarf we felt quite at home. The place was deserted except for the bar man who initially seemed disinterested by our presence. A few drinks later and he was introducing us to some of the local brands and was more than happy to entertain our weary conversation. I've read about the Italian football fanatics that fall under the banner of 'Ultras,' and perhaps it was somewhat fortunate that it wasn't a busy night, and no questions were asked. Perhaps naivety plays a great part in being a stranger in paradise, only the locals ever know the dangerous streets, the poisonous creatures and the local train routes. If catching the wrong train wasn't bad enough, we also caught the wrong bus the following day. The bus stop to the city centre was just around the corner from the hotel. Stupid as it may seem we got on the wrong bus around the wrong corner. The bus that we got on took us on a journey that meandered across the seven surrounding hills of Rome. Realising once more that we were now heading further away from the city centre and that old story about Romans building straight roads wasn't true. Fortunately, another passenger informed us in good English, that we were arriving at a large bus depot and that we should get off there and ask for some information regarding a bus to the city. The bus depot was quite large for a terminal in the middle of the countryside, and we managed to find an information help desk. We were all slightly perplexed when we were told that no buses that went back to the city came into this depot, but if we walked about ten minutes down the road, we would see a small bus stop that had an hourly bus going to the city centre. We stood under a small yellow bus shelter on a deserted country road surrounded by fields and hedgerows. There were no houses in sight and the road consisted of a long continuous bend as far as the eye could see. The weather had changed, and we were now covered in a blanket of smouldering grey clouds that threatened a heavy downpour at any minute. We stood silent and waited, watching the most distant point in the road for any signs of a vehicle. Half an hour had past, and we had probably seen two cars go by, we still found it remarkable that we were not standing in the bus depot. Suddenly in the distance but not in sight we could hear sirens wailing and the screeching of tyres skidding across the road surface. Within a split second the wailing started coming from both directions and increasingly closer. From our right hand direction came a speeding blue saloon car which was being chased by three other cars. The other cars we later understood were unmarked police cars, each with a blue flashing light manually stuck to their rooftops. From the other direction came two other police cars side by side leaving no were to go. The evading car pulled up gently at the bus stop and the occupants were quickly dragged to the roadside by the frenetic police officers. We had ringside seats, and everything unfolded around us as if we weren't even there. They glanced at us occasionally but said nothing and we carried on watching the events hardly daring to move. Some popcorn and a bag of sweets would have been ideal, and it was remarkable that we were never asked to stand aside. At this point I don't think any of us wanted the bus to arrive. The officers opened the boot to the car in front of us and started to remove several large polythene bags that we guessed must have been drugs. I don't think they would have sent this many cars to stop a shoplifter from Sainsburys. With the felons handcuffed and in the back of another car, they all drove off calmly, still not having spoken a word. The blue car remained abandoned at the bus stop, no doubt to be picked up and dusted down later. We didn't have long to wait before our bus arrived and we stepped onto it having felt like we'd been extras in a movie.

CHAPTER 19

Miami Strife

The name Miami derives from the original name for the tribal people who lived in this area before European colonisation. The Maiyami people have long since disappeared and the holiday hotspot is populated by many people who fled from Cuba during the 1959 Cuban revolution. My wife and I flew into Miami in order to board a cruise ship visiting the Caribbean. The Norwegian Pearl was due to set sail from the port the day after we had landed so we didn't get much time to visit the popular tourist spots. For many of us, Miami first came to our attention in 1984 through Don Johnson and the detective series Miami Vice. Featuring its famous Art Deco buildings that pays homage to the nineteen twenties and thirties. It also boasts the third highest skyline in America along with one of the world's busiest ports. Being part of the sunshine state of Florida, Miami offers an idyllic place to live, work and take a holiday. On our first trip to Miami, we stayed at the Sheraton Miami airport hotel, which was a stone's throw from the airport runways and overlooked the Melrose International golf club. This hotel was part of the cruise package, and it was the kind of hotel that people pass through briefly on their way to other destinations. After putting our suitcases in the room, we took the lift from the top floor down to the reception to grab a drink at the bar. As we reached the ground floor the lift doors opened to reveal that we were at least three feet below the ground floor level. The doors hadn't opened fully, and we were greeted by the manager of the hotel who asked if we thought we could manage to climb out.

Somewhat startled by this i jumped up and reached down to give my wife a hand up. It was of those 'did that really just happen,' moments? If you read Wikipedia's list of elevator accidents, you might never step foot in a lift again. Decapitations, people cut in half and a whole list of gruesome deaths can be attributed to the good old elevator. Intact, we made our way to the hotel garden that was adjacent to a water way that looked similar to a canal in the Uk. On the opposite bank was the fairway of a golf course that was lined with tall palm trees along the fringe and lots of shimmering lakes in the distance. Sitting motionless on the opposite bank were several large Green Iguanas basking in the late evening sun. The large males are easy to recognise by their distinctive bright orange skin, which apparently changes colour to attract females, think seventies disco. Although tired from the long flight we decided to go on a walk with the aim of finding some shops to pick up supplies. After leaving the hotel, we took a right turn onto thirty seventh avenue, a wide road which divided the golf course from a suburb of one storey houses or bungalows as we call them in the UK. Ten minutes into our journey we noticed a couple of police officers in a heated debate with some of the residents. I must admit whenever I'm in America I can't help but think guns, shootings and gang warfare. Seemed only natural that we continued at a brisk pace to the next junction and made another right turn. Realising that there were no shops in the vicinity, it would make sense to follow the road clockwise which should in theory lead us back to the hotel. The light was beginning to fade quickly, and the pavement was becoming decidedly narrow, until eventually tailed off and became rough dry ground. The fence surrounding the golf course was at least twenty feet high in order to protect motorists from odd stray golf ball. The most sensible thing to do now would be to turn back but i insisted we continued forwards. The next right turn brought us on to forty second avenue and this looked like the M6 but five times the size. We could see the Sheraton hotel sign in the distance but there wasn't a pathway. The only way to negotiate the waterway was to use the huge flyover. The relentless traffic and no hard shoulder made it far too dangerous to even consider. As we were about to turn about face and retrace our steps, I noticed a hole in the wired fence, big enough for us to climb through. I told my wife that by cutting across the golf course we could half the return journey. The thought of trespassing never entered my mind and the desire to get back to the safety of the hotel was all I could think of. Although a little reluctant my wife agreed, and we pushed through the gap in the damaged fence. Standing in the dark in a remote corner of a Miami golf course was not my smartest decision. Little did we know that there was a small concrete bridge just out of sight of where we were stood. Had we have spotted it; we could have crossed the canal and been back to the hotel in minutes. Being a keen golfer, I headed straight for the club house as I assumed that's where the nearest exit would be. It meant that we needed to walk the entire width of the golf course in what was almost zero visibility. The lights of the motorway and the distant neighbourhoods were a soft hue of yellow almost like someone holding a candle at the back of a church. I'd spotted the club house when we'd first set off so in my mind's eye, I had a good positional sense of the direction to take. The noise of the cars faded as we approached the centre of the course, and we could now hear the high pitched shrills and low stifled grunts of the Miami wildlife. Mockingbirds and Limpkins making all the background noises you would need for a horror film. The smooth concrete path took us between two large expanses of water surrounded by small shrubs and the odd Cluster of trees. Every so often a loud splashing sound came from somewhere in the distance and I put it down to fish jumping clear of the water to catch passing flies. That was until my wife pointed at the sign saying, 'beware of alligators.' I'd read about golfers going missing on the course and in some cases, it had been put down to an alligator attack. Recently at the time of writing, there have been reports in the Miami Herald of large alligators roaming freely around certain golf courses. We quickly upped the pace and must have looked like Dorothy and the cowardly lion as we held on to each other and quick stepped down the grey path. It may not have been the Emerald city, but the club house was a welcome relief. Suddenly a voice called out from the darkness, 'what the hell y'all doing here?' Explaining that he was about to lock up and somewhat bemused by the stupid Brits, the caretaker let us back out onto the main road. In the distance we could see the red lights of the hotel signage and we were now only a fifteen minute walk away. The ironic thing about being lost in Miami was the fact that we were never actually lost. Cut off maybe, stranded perhaps, but never truly lost. Without a guide or google maps or any kind of map, we are all lost to begin with. Whether it's walking through Corfu old town or visiting a remote island in the Galapagos, were all lost until you find an Irish bar. My wife nearly managed to miss her own daughter's wedding due to being lost and for once i was blameless. Arriving at the ceremony in tears with seconds to spare an elderly gentleman had pointed her in the right direction as she frantically dashed around Central park looking for the Belvedere Castle. Think about it, a square shaped park surrounded by tall buildings, how can anyone get lost? Central Park is quite vast, and it covers around 1.3 square miles. Designed by Frederick Olmsted who based it on Birkenhead park after visiting Liverpool in 1850. Basically, you had a woman born in the centre of Liverpool lost in a park in the centre of New York, which was designed on a park in Liverpool.

Being lost on holiday is bad enough, but if there's someone around who can speak your language then at least you can get directions. Being lost in an area where English is not commonly spoken as a second language you can get into all kinds of bother. I'm always amazed at how so many Europeans go to the trouble of learning English as their second language and yet us brits can't be bothered getting to grips with any other language. To be fair it's hard enough trying to communicate with some people in our own country given the amount of dialects we have in Britain.

They say the people in Europe appreciate it when we give their language a try and forgive our shortcomings. I went through a phase of trying to learn Spanish and as much as i tried, it just wouldn't sink in. Me no habla Espanyol to this day, however, i did give it a try on a couple of occasions and both ended in disaster. The first time I thought I'd give my Spanish a try was at a MacDonalds in Malaga, were i ordered eighty eight burgers for four people. The manager was called over and i stood there with a stupid grin smiling proudly. I think the person who'd taken my order, had tried to explain what id asked for but didn't speak any English. I couldn't believe this person was working in a Macdonald's and couldn't speak English, even if we were in Spain. Should be the first question at the interview. The manager intervened and explained much to my embarrassment that they don't have a tray big enough to carry eighty eight burgers. Another occasion when i killed the Spanish language, was during a golf trip to Mijas, also in the province of Malaga. Four blokes squeezed tightly into a hire car with four sets of golf clubs heading for Mijas golf course, what could be better. We knew from the panoramic view that we were not in the right place and to see buzzards circle the skies and land below us rubber stamped that we were to high and officially lost. We were supposed to be somewhere near the coast and not driving through the actual village of Mijas, which is perched 1,476 feet above sea level on a mountain side. Beautiful, whitewashed houses line the narrow streets and its certainly not the place to be driving on a market day. But as we inched our way down Caril street, we were not only lost but also surrounded by goats and sheep who were all over us like they were security for the president. I spotted an old guy walking with his hands behind his back, bent over slightly and wearing an old cloth cap. 'Perdon senor, buenos dias, donde esta de la campo de golf Mijas por favour?' Sounded great, bet the lads are well impressed, i thought. The old guy leaned into the window and gave us a big smile, revealing the last remaining tooth in his head, 'ah golf, si, si.' I realised that my efforts had been translated perfectly and all had been understood. Except this old fella wasn't about to reply in English now, was he? I received an avalanche of Spanish chit chat combined with an uncontrollable spray of saliva every five words. To my reckoning i heard, 'eesa, ooosa, golfio, si, mueble, quatro, stupido and other words that meant absolutely nothing to my untrained ears. When he finished giving directions he stood back and gave us a cheery wave saying adios and waving his cap and pointing in the direction of the buzzards. 'What did he say,' asked the other lads? I shrugged my shoulders and said, 'not a fucking clue, but I'm covered in spit.' A few hundred yards later we pulled up next to a Spanish police offer who was standing on a box controlling the traffic. I asked in English if he knew where Mijas golf course was and could he give us directions. 'Yes, he replied in near perfect English, 'end of this road, turn right, down the hill for a few miles, can't miss it.' He was Spanish, no doubting that, but his English accent was so good, I could have been talking to Hugh Bonneville in Downton Abbey.

Playing golf around southern Spain is perhaps one of the most enjoyable sporting experiences I've ever had. The abundance of superb courses which are manicured to perfection, combined with a large helping of blue skies and sunshine, make for a perfect day out. Before playing Mijas we had opted for another course which was up in the hills. Having met up in Manchester airport at four in the morning we knew it was going to be a long day. The drive to Lauro golf course was to be no different from all the other journeys we made that week. We were lost for a short time up yet another mountain but always managed to get back on track. There was no Google maps back then and as arrogant as it may seem, we thought four blokes in one car would be the equivalent of a mighty testosterone sat nav. We failed to find our way first time to any course, and we were late for every tee off. In the mid-day heat, we trudged wearily but enthusiastically around this particular hilly golf course drenched in sweat but loving every minute. As we arrived at the ninth hole the heat and the tiredness were beginning to take its toll and the energy levels were draining. On the edge of the course to our right some new villas were being built and were nearly close to completion. A hundred yards away was a bright orange crane lifting what looked like blocks of paving stones towards some men who were probably creating the pavements between the villas. Leaning precariously out of the cab door of the crane was the operator whose features were recognisable even from so high up and at a distance. He wore a high vis jacket and a white safety hat; his appearance was rotund with dark skin and a thick black moustache. The crane had dropped its load and he now had time to watch us from up high and started to shout to us in a comical tone. 'Get in the hole, get in the hole,' he shouted loudly in broken English. This is a much maligned statement irritating many golf enthusiasts and is not really welcome. We smiled and gave him a wave, as watching some people hitting a golf ball was probably a welcome distraction when sitting alone high up in a cabin all day. Me and my brother in law hit two good shots to the Green but when my friend Mark sliced his ball ferociously off the tee, it took to the air like an Exocet missile. It smashed violently against the open door of the cab just missing the driver, sending him into waves of abuse. 'You fukeeeen eeediots, yua tryana kill me or what? Yousa shouldn't be on a fukeeeen golfa course. I come down there I fukeeeen killa you.' We collapsed in heaps of laughter as he comically shook his first. There was no point in trying to continue, we called it a day and went to the bar. A few drinks later and we were back on the road.

Today's mobile phones carry more technology than NASA possessed when sending rockets to the moon. Satellite navigation, Google Earth and just the fact you can talk to someone from the most remote places on the planet, means it's impossible to be truly lost. Imagine if today's phones had happened thirty years earlier.

Bonnie Tyler's 1974 pop song 'Lost in France,' wouldn't have been written or the 2004 TV series 'Lost,' wouldn't be feasible. Seventy two passengers crash onto a mysterious island and stay there for over a hundred episodes, never going to happen. If they had a mobile phone of today's standards they'd be rescued within an hour . They may have to walk about a bit to get a signal and once connected go through the options of, 'press one, to 'report an incident, 'then 'press two,' to 'request a call back,' but help would soon be on its way. While waiting to be rescued they would also receive a couple of PPI calls and of course 'you've been in an accident,' call.

Being lost only confirms that we have a sense of belonging. We like the feeling of being in a safe environment and the sense of security that this brings, and yet there is a sense of adventure when traveling into the unknown. We enjoy that moment of exploration as long as we can get home in time for tea. Everything you do in life is centred on getting home. 'Around the World in Eighty Days,' was the Jules Verne book that captured the world's imagination. Phileas Fogg faced all kinds of adversity including being lost.' But he made sure that he got back to London to win his bet and therefore have enough money to pay his gas bill and television licence. Modern day travel allows us to hop around the planet in much shorter time and today we think nothing of getting on a plane to visit a European city for the weekend.

A shorter journey that took me on my one and only visit to Ireland, involved nothing more than a three hour ferry crossing. During my years working as a welder in a powder coating factory a few of my colleagues decided that it would be good idea for us to spend a weekend in Dublin. When the day came, twelve of us jumped aboard the 'Sea Cat,' in Liverpool and headed off into the Irish Sea. Twelve men aged between thirty and fifty carrying overnight bags and hangers with jackets on. One of us had managed to find a hotel that would accept all of us for a very cheap rate. This included breakfast and a bus to and from the dockside in Dublin. When we arrived at the hotel located somewhere in the city centre, we were given a warm welcome. The hotel looked clean and better than we had imagined. After checking us in, the proprietor of the hotel, a lady I'd say in her mid-forties' asked us to follow her as she opened a side door beyond the reception area. She led us up a flight of stairs that started with a carpet, but by the time we had reached the top floor it was bare wooden steps. This staircase was unusual as in the fact that it didn't have any openings to any of the other floors. 'This way boys,' she said with the authority of somebody who'd done this many times before. On the fifth floor she opened the only door that existed at the top of this gloomily lit staircase. We filed in like the seven dwarfs being led by Snow White, except we were a little taller and more like the dirty dozen. 'Take your pick, 'she said pointing at the beds, 'breakfast at seven but I'll serve you up to ten as long as your packed and ready to go.' She turned and left the room, saying something along the lines of 'keep the feckin noise down,' leaving us to fight over which bed we were having. Eleven beds in one huge dilapidated but spacious room, and one bed in a small private room near to the doorway. Adjacent to this small room was a shower and a leaky toilet in what must have been a converted cupboard. We'd drawn straws for the little side room after we'd booked the hotel through the Liverpool Echo. It was kind of fitting that the eldest of our party had won the right to sleep there and George was delighted he'd drawn the shortest straw. The smaller room was as dreary as its counterpart and from the middle of the ceiling a long black wire with a bare lightbulb hung just a couple of feet above the mattress. The rest of us threw our bags onto whatever bed we could claim first and realised that it was impossible to fully stretch out due to the size of the bed frames. There was a single wooden framed window that let in daylight through a filthy pair of bright orange curtains. The room had anaglypta wallpaper that had been painted over a thousand times and was now sporting a shade of Dijon mustard. There was no visible signs of heating apart from the light bulbs and the damp had caused the decor to peel away from the top of the walls. Undeterred we set off for an afternoon of drinking on the famous O'Connell street. It wasn't long before we found our way into a lively sports bar and a few hours later we made our way to the Temple Bar area. When hunger finally diverted us away from the Guinness, there wasn't any restaurants that would let us in without having previously booked. However, all was not lost, and we were delighted when a Chinese 'all you can eat,' buffet style restaurant happily accommodated us around two large tables. I feel they may have regretted this decision as they struggled to keep the buffet dishes topped up for other guests as we demolished the contents like a swarm of locusts. Refuelled, we hit the bars again somehow managing to find room to guzzle endless rounds of Guinness until we eventually decided to head back towards the direction of the hotel. The glorious weather had now turned into sporadic heavy showers as the evening sky disappeared above the streetlights. We joined a queue of people who looked to be going into a night club but soon found out it was a long queue for a cash machine hidden out of sight around the corner. We found another bar that was guarded by two thick set doormen with their customary black jackets and bow ties. They stood above us on a flight of small steps that led to a doorway with a 'Welcome to Kelly's,' sign above it. 'You can't come in,' we were told sternly by one of the doormen. 'Why not,' asked George, our spokesman and elder statesman? 'Regulars only,' came the reply and without argument we were ready to turn away. George however wasn't about to give up. 'Look lads, we're not looking to cause trouble, we just want a quiet drink somewhere out of the rain.' The doormen weren't interested and looked down at George and calmly said, 'like we said, regulars only.' George who was a sharp as a tac looked up and politely asked, 'how do we become regulars?' The two doormen stared at each other blankly, as if hit with a maths question. 'By fucking off back to Liverpool,' came the answer more sternly. We took it as a final answer and set off once more in the direction of our hotel. A passer-by had overheard us at Kelly's doorstep and informed us that there was a small pub two streets down if we were looking for last orders. Some of us dashed off in the direction of the pub while others took shelter in shop doorways from the onset of the heavy rain. Those of us who arrived first were greeted by a nervous bar tender who immediately asked us not to cause trouble. We were soon followed by another three of our party and then some others who just couldn't be bothered to run. 'We don't want no trouble boys, that's all I'm asking,' repeated the barman, 'Guinness on its way.' The narrow pub had someone playing a piano in the far corner of the room and all the seats were taken. It became apparent that we were one short, 'where's Ronnie,' asked one of the lads? Ronnie who was easily around six foot four in height and strong with it, was the last to arrive. He ducked slightly as he came through the small door and stood there soaked to the skin but smiling. The piano had stopped just after our arrival and the rest of the pub had fallen into an eerie hum of low chatter. It seemed that the other patrons were now listening to our conversations and watching to see how we'd behave. 'Oh Jesus, he's a big fella,' the barman called out. 'I don't want any trouble from the big man d yer hear?' Ronnie was a strong as an Ox and could lift you off your feet quite easily, but he was also a gentle mild mannered soul. 'The big fella wanting a Guinness too, I better ask?' The bartender held up an empty glass towards Ronnie waiting for a nod of approval. 'I'll have a Malibu and coke if that's alright with you and stick one of those paper brollies in it, I'll use it for the way home,' replied Ronnie and the place including the regulars completely fell apart. The nervous barman was the only person who didn't laugh, he just stared in disbelief.

The hotel stairs felt like the north side of K2, and we all fell up every step. Pissed, rotten, hammered, wrecked, slammed, leathered, smashed, but no Snow White. The room was absolutely freezing and the duvets on each bed were as thin as paper. Throughout the night it became a steady traipse of traffic back and forth to the toilet and those that bothered to flush only added more water to the already soaked bathroom floor. Each time someone put the toilet light on, the bulb in the small room just above Georges head came on simultaneously. It must have been on the same circuit, and this drove George to insanity. In the morning he remarked how he'd seen a captured SAS soldier undergo the same treatment to cause sleep deprivation. On the way back to the boat the following morning we were stopped by a local man who asked us 'why do you want to come to Dublin?' We came for the craic, and the Irish hospitality we told him. He looked at us and said, 'is that right, see Dublin it's Liverpool with some water in between, wasted ya fuckin' time and money so you have.' He was right, we hadn't visited anything historical or heard any Irish music. We'd learnt nothing about Irish history, and we knew nothing about the events that took place in O'Connell street during the Easter rising. We'd drank copious amounts of Belgian lager, shovelled down a Chinese meal and watched the English premier league in a sports bar. Back in Liverpool many people had spent the night in the numerous Irish bars in the centre of town, listening to touring Irish bands and singers.

CHAPTER 20

Roll With It

When travelling abroad it's important to remember that other countries have different beliefs and customs. It's quite easy to offend without meaning to and in some countries the consequences can be severe. It's illegal for French people to kiss on a train and You can't chew gum in Singapore. You also can't hike naked in Switzerland and it's illegal for men to belly dance in Egypt, which is a shame as I definitely had the last two on my bucket list. Don't get caught stealing in Iran, as the punishment is to have four fingers amputated from your right hand, not your whole hand as many some would believe. Still a very severe punishment indeed and you can say goodbye to knitting a tea cosy and belting out 'Pin Ball Wizard,' on the piano. When arriving in the Gili Islands for the first time we were welcomed by the hotel staff with lots of polite bowing and hands clasped in a prayer position. My wife was asked to take a seat in the open air reception where she took responsibility for checking us all in. My son leaned over his mother's shoulder and in a very low whisper told us both that it was considered rude not to take a sip of any drink or a bite of any food that we may be offered. Moments later we were more than happy to accept the colourful cocktail drinks we'd been offered and politely took a sip. Whilst my wife was busy handing over our passports and signing some paperwork, a young Balinese lady came towards us in full traditional costume, carrying a tray of small rolled up flannels. They had been chilled and contained a small fragrance of lemon that were perfect for cooling ones forehead and neck. She bowed and offered one to my wife, who was busy giving passport details to the manager. She thanked the young lady and popped the flannel straight into her mouth. She thought it was some kind of rice cake or sushi and took a strong bite on the chilled white cloth, before tentatively placing it back down onto the table in front of the astonished manager. Her teeth marks were embedded in the cloth like a dental impression but were soon removed quickly on her reddening face.

It's incidents like these that give us our nostalgia moments when getting together with friends . You don't go back to the office and tell your mates and colleagues about the great view you had from the hotel balcony. They won't be jealous of the photo of the lasagne at Gino's Italian restaurant in Benidorm. If you haven't already figured this out, let me tell you something you should know and it's a horrible truth. No one is interested in your holiday photos; they absolutely don't give a flying fuck. No one cares about your amazing hotel and who you met. They will smile and try to look interested, but ask yourself this, do they really want to see you standing next to the fountain of goats milk? That's the whole reason we have 'Trip Advisor, to find out for ourselves. My late uncle used to think we were having a great time viewing his holiday slides on one of those old slide projectors' during the seventies. 'This is me and your aunty Madge outside the tent by lake Geneva,' he'd proudly announce, and his hostages would smile and say 'lovely.' There's only so many times you can say, 'looks marvellous that Uncle James,' before realising that you genuinely do have Tourette's syndrome and burst out with 'shove them fuckin' slides were the sun doesn't shine, I'm bored shitless. Being ten years of age i thought better of it. What really would have grabbed our attention is, something along the lines of, 'this is where me and your aunty Madge were kidnapped by the rebel alliance and were forced to do some gun running between Bognor Regis and Burkina Faso.

Lying on a beach and sunbathing all day long is some peoples idea of total bliss, and it counts as their number one holiday activity. This always reminds me of the Marine Iguanas in the David Attenborough's 'Life on Earth,' series. Moving slowly across Levante beach in Benidorm i can imagine his whispering tone describing the statuesque humans. 'Every so often they race across the sand lifting their feet rapidly to avoid burning their tender soles.' *Our soles* or human feet as they are better known, rarely see daylight and without flip flops the dash to the ocean is the equivalent of running on hot coals, thankfully we get to quench them in salty water.'

Getting sun burnt down under was something to be wary of when we visited Australia, so when my son told me we were going to a place that has no sunlight I was quite intrigued. Just down the coast from Perth is the city of Fremantle which up until 1991 was the location for Australia's largest prison. Built in 1850 the prison is famous for the labyrinth of tunnels that were bored deep into the rock beneath its foundations. Created by the prisoners under the watchful eye of the wardens, they reach a depth of well over twenty metres. At the base of the tunnels, there is a multitude of chambers that are filled with fresh water which can only be navigated by small two man boats known as Punts. The prisoners were pressured into digging through this solid rock in order to access fresh water for the city's expanding population above. For every yard the prison gang dug out they chipped a little time off their sentence. Getting into the protective clothing and being hooked up with ropes and clips made me question the sanity of the whole experience. My hard hat wobbled from side to side uncontrollably as I climbed down a steel ladder into what felt like the abyss. For my son who climbs communication towers hundreds of feet high, it was like a busman's holiday. He had already clipped himself up with all the gear before the safety instructor had arrived. They knew instantly that he knew the ropes but still professionally checked his tackle, no pun intended. It took a lot of energy and swapping from ladder to ladder to get to the base of the tunnels and I remember thinking, what's it's going to be like climbing back out. Eight of us including the guide met up at the base of the decent and huddled in a confined space where it was impossible to stand upright. There were small lights attached sporadically to the rock face every couple of metres giving a warm glow to the tunnels that disappeared into the distance. The guide began our journey by asking us all to be as quiet as possible and to turn off our headlights. He then turned all the tunnel lights off using a mains switch and said, 'this is now as pitch black as you will ever experience in your life and at this level you will hear no sound, not even the vibration of the heavy traffic above.'

I can't say that was exactly awe inspiring , I'm half deaf and blind at the best of times, but when he switched the light back on, we were shocked to see his face snarled up in excruciating pain. He held on to his chest and mumbled the words 'I think I'm in trouble.' We all laughed and thought, good joke, yep, we'd all be a bit helpless if this was true. But he carried on holding onto his chest and was struggling to speak. He managed to take out his walkie talkie from a top pocket and we heard him speak to his contact on the surface. 'Ten six Charlie, ten six Charlie, casualty, i say casualty, immediate evac, over.' We all knew at this point he wasn't kidding. 'Ten six Charlie understood,' what's the code Steve, over?' Steve our guide was now lying on his back breathing heavily, 'it's me Barry, code black, I've got cardiac problems, need stretcher lift asap.' Surely to god I wasn't going to do my third stint of CPR in a bloody tunnel under a prison? Me and my son were the closest to Steve in a positional sense, but would you fucking believe it, we had a Chinese doctor in our party? I gladly shuffled to one side to let her attend to Steve, and I'm now convinced that Drs are like rats. There's an old saying that 'your never more than a couple of yards away from a rat,' such are their prevalence. I now believe you can say, 'you are never more than a few yards away from a doctor.' It's too coincidental that there were doctors on both of the flights I was on, when people had chest issues. Within a few minutes a rescue team had appeared carrying a stretcher, the type you see on a helicopter rescue. I was surprised at how quickly they had our guide strapped in and was hauling him up the ladders at great speed. The unfortunate Steve was replaced by a younger man who asked us if we were happy to continue. Concerned as we were for Steve, we continued on our journey, minus the Chinese doctor. The convicts who volunteered to dig these claustrophobic tunnels, must have been bordering on insanity. Even with modern ladders and electric lighting the cramped experience is truly unsettling. To have climbed down some rickety wooden ladders using oil lamps and constantly fearing the possibility of a tunnel collapse, must have been totally nerve shredding. Thankfully Steve wasn't given a death sentence when escaping from the prison tunnels to a hospital bed and happy to say went on to serve a few more years in prison, so to speak.

If climbing down a giant hole in the ground doesn't light your candle, then you should try a bit of sand surfing in Lancelin, north of Perth. In a moment of bravado, I dragged a sand board to the highest sand dune we could find in this mountainous dessert landscape. These are no ordinary dunes they are steep and difficult to climb. From ground level some of them must be fifty feet high with a one hundred and fifty feet slope. Foolishly I decided to stand up rather than sit down, having watched my son glide effortlessly to the bottom of the hill. As I hurtled down the sand dune at an immense speed I felt like an absolute dude. Showing perfect balance for a guy of over fifty, I was sure my son was looking up the hill, thinking, 'my dad is one helluva guy.' Then just yards from safety I lost my balance and nose-dived into the sand like cannon ball hitting a bowl of custard. Except this white sand felt like concrete and if you'd have told me I'd broken every bone in my body I'd have believed you. The pain from head to toe was immense and yet by some miracle i was still in one piece. When it comes to this type of activity, I'd like to impart the most valuable tip you will read. Surfing is for the guys with a six pack, long hair and should never be attempted by anyone with grey hair, grandchildren or by blokes trying to look cool in front of their kids. Better tip: Just wear a bandana, sunglasses and get a high powered motorbike.

Australia or at least the west coast of Australia is a beautiful part of the world. Life seems more slower and certainly warmer in and around Perth. My son, sister and brother in law, live on the outskirts of the city and they were keen to show us the beaches and the perks associated with leaving the Uk. I had no intention of putting my big toe in the water such is my fear of being lunch for a great white shark. I did ride across the Swan River on the back of a jet ski with my son which was a marvellous experience. The river which starts some fifty miles inland, works its way into an open estuary before joining the sea through the Fremantle harbour. Situated twenty three kilometres off the coast of Fremantle is Rottnest Island which is famous for its abundance of sharks including the notorious Great White. As we twisted and turned at high speed across the bay, I kept looking down at the water thinking what if I fall off? I shouldn't have been concerned as there has only ever been four attacks recorded in the Swan river, but I sure wasn't up for being the fifth. As a teenager growing up through the seventies, Spielberg's 'Jaws,' became imprinted on everybody's mind even if you lived miles from the sea. I went to watch this film in Southport a seaside town in the northwest of England where the chances of being killed by a great white shark could be compared to that of being killed by a mermaid. It didn't matter, I was in Australia, and they were out there waiting for me, swimming somewhere beyond the beach. To celebrate my nieces birthday, my brother in law had hired a houseboat for the day and with great skill and a bottle of beer in his hand he navigated us carefully down the river to another wide expanse of water. In fact, it was so large it was similar to a lake in many aspects. My niece and her boyfriend were happy to relax in the jacuzzi at the back of the boat while my brother in law, his father and my son were happy to fish at the front of the boat. I was amused that I was somehow catching fish while the others were catching crabs. I caught a puffer fish which blew up like some kind of angry conker shell flaring out its thorny spikes. 'There's sharks in here dad, Bronze Whalers and Bull Sharks,' my son began to deliberately plant a seed in my mind. I'd seen photos of my son catching a large shark from the beach, so I sort of half believed him. Twenty minutes later my fishing rod bent in half with amazing force. I was shocked and terrified in one heart-stopping moment. 'My god I think it's a shark,' I called out to the others. My rod and line swung tightly around the edge of the houseboat which was a perfect rectangle. 'You've got one dad,' shouted my son triumphantly, 'it must have swallowed a smaller fish as you caught it.' The spool on my rod screamed as I wound the handle on the reel. 'It's too big, I need a bigger rod.' I suppose it was almost as iconic as, 'were gonna need a bigger boat.' But as I leaned carefully around the corner edge of the boat my catch had surfaced minus a dorsal fin. My nieces boyfriend had jumped off the back of the boat, grabbed my line and swam behind the boat, keeping out of sight. To my embarrassment I really thought I'd caught a shark, much to the amusement of all the other passengers.

Australia taught me one thing, I'm not cool, not in the slightest. It is a place that cares little for people with an ego or for anyone going out to impress. It threw off its shackles and inhibitions a long time ago and created a society of people who value time well spent. They don't say 'good morning,' they say 'g'day,' and why not, it's better to have a good day, it lasts longer?

CHAPTER 21

A Greek Tragedy

This next chapter is without doubt the saddest holiday story I have ever heard. I feel it can be told now as it happened some thirty years ago, and it shouldn't cause any further upset. Just in case the people whom this story relates to are still alive and there's every chance, I have changed all the names associated with this tragic occurrence. I remember this story for two reasons, the first being, that the people who were telling me this story were doing so less than seventy two hours after they'd set off on an eagerly awaited holiday. They were absolutely destroyed as they explained their nightmare journey and their own Greek tragedy. Secondly because I fell apart laughing as they told me. It was wrong to laugh, and I could only apologise and make some excuse about it sounding so ridiculous that it became comical. Janice and Malcolm had booked a ten day holiday to a Greek resort that they had never seen or been to before. It was a spare of the moment decision and the girl in the holiday shop had promoted it so well. They'd paid their deposit and began to prepare for their holiday and in conversation told their neighbour and friend Eileen about their planned trip. Eileen, who was disabled and used a wheelchair, remarked how lucky they were and wished that she could go on a family holiday someday. Perhaps just a passing remark, but the next day Janice knocked on Eileen's door and did what no one else in the right mind would do and invited her along. Now this was extremely generous, not in the money sense as Eileen would be paying for herself but in the fact that Janice was taking on something she knew little about. Having a neighbour in a wheelchair is nothing extraordinary but you don't ask questions about how they get dressed in the morning or get in and out of bed or go to the toilet. The day of the holiday arrived and Janice, Malcolm and their two children climbed onboard the luggagbus waiting to take them to the airport. They had omitted to inform the luggabus company that one of their party was disabled and so began lesson one of the difficulties that people in wheelchairs face constantly. The driver understanding the dilemma, admirably helped Malcolm lift Eileen plus wheelchair into what should have been the luggage space at the back of the bus. This then meant transferring the suitcases from the boot space onto the bus seats. After some unusual adjustments they finally made their way to Manchester airport. A slightly undignified journey for Eileen staring out at the traffic behind them as they travelled along the M6. The check in apparently went smoothly as did the boarding onto the aircraft. Janice had informed the holiday company about Eileen's disability when calling to amend the booking and they were aware of a passenger in a wheelchair as part of their party. I have no idea where they landed in Greece but once they'd picked up their luggage, they made their way to another desk to register for their transfer to their hotel. Another struggle ensued as Eileen was hoisted into yet another minibus, but their next destination was not to a hotel. Instead, they found themselves arriving at a small port. 'We take you by boat to the island,' they were told by another person who met them off the bus. 'We were not aware of the chair,' said the hotel rep who smiled with a degree of awkwardness. The boat, Malcolm informed me was nothing more than a local fishing boat and he argued that to get Eileen down the concrete steps was going to be dangerous, worse still, onto a boat that was pitching to and fro. Somehow, they managed to get Eileen down the stairs and onto the small fishing boat cabin which doubled as a passenger ferry. The heat was taking its toll and tempers were beginning to flare and the only saving grace for Malcolm was the thought of standing at the bar having an ice cold and well-earned beer. After a short crossing they arrived at an island which had a landing stage, so getting Eileen back onto dry land was a lot easier. Finally, they arrived at the hotel reception lathered in sweat but grateful for the air conditioning. Once again eyebrow's we're beginning to raise as the hotel reception started to chat feverishly between themselves throwing the odd bemused glance at the party of English people who were taking little notice. 'Madam, you have not informed us of a wheelchair in your party.' Not the greatest description of a person on holiday but the shit was about to hit the fan as they say. 'Yes, I bloody did,' I told them when I amended the booking.' Janice was the type who could come across as very 'straight forward,' and from what she told me, the hotel staff were not intimidated or overly concerned. They were told that there were no rooms available on the ground floor of the hotel and that their accommodation was a bungalow a small distance away from the hotel. In fact, it was up a winding set of steps to the top of a small hill. They would need to wait until tomorrow for a hotel room to become available on the ground floor, before they could be moved.

Knowing that it would be important to keep the hotel staff onside until another room was found Janice and Malcolm reluctantly accepted the key to the bungalow on the hill. Malcolm and Janice were left to drag, carry and fight their way to the top of the hill with the poor unfortunate Eileen feeling terribly helpless and the cause of all their woes.

Thankfully the hotel staff brought up the suitcases and now they could get washed and changed and out of their sweat laden clothes. It was late in the evening and Malcolm suggested they go down to the hotel bar near the pool and get some food and a drink. Eileen who by this time had probably had enough of being carted about declined the offer and said she was having an early night. Feeling slightly guilty but needing some sanity Janice, Malcolm and the kids made their way down to the hotel pool bar to get some refreshments and a well-earned drink. They told me that there was a party atmosphere well under way and lots of guests were chatting and get to know each other. It wasn't long before Malcolm had downed a few beers and found himself on the karaoke singing, 'always look on the bright side of life.' He showed me the photo of this poignant moment and it has stuck with me ever since. Not drunk but exhausted and tired they made their way back to their rooms for some well-earned rest. In the morning Janice was awake first and started reading through some hotel literature regarding places to eat and possibly get some breakfast. At this point she thought she'd check on Eileen who didn't reply even when Janice knocked loudly on her bedroom door. This was concerning and Janice tried again sometime later but still no answer. She told Malcolm that she was concerned, so they tentatively went into her room where they found that she was still in bed. Worse still, she was dead. Admittedly I could have put this more sensitively and said she had passed away or something more appropriate, but this is how it was told to me. Janice took up the story and gave her rendition of how she recollected the conversation with her husband. Word for word.

'Fuck Malcolm I think she's dead.'

How do you know she's dead Janice, she might be a heavy sleeper?

She's fucking cold Malcolm and it's fucking roasting in here.

Don't fucking tell me she's dead Janice, not now, were on holiday.

Well, she's not fucking breathing for starters, she's slate fucking grey and you may not have noticed but she hasn't fucking said good morning yet.'

Malcolm and Janice had to go down to the reception and explain their predicament and it wasn't long before the police arrived. They in turn called for an ambulance and Malcolm and Janice had to make statements. Later that day, Janice was asked to go the local mortuary not only to identify the body but was also asked to dress it. They then had to help arrange transportation to the UK and sign the documents to allow the body to be flown back to England. They cut their own holiday short and I'm not sure how they became aware of this, but they flew back on the same plane as Eileen who was unfortunately in the hold.

Malcolm looked at me and said, 'I was singing 'always look on the bright side of life,' hours before finding a dead body in the room next to me.' They'd been neighbours for years without so much as a hiccup and yet one holiday to Greece and the Gods conspired to wreak havoc. You may say how can you find this funny its almost offensive? People do actually die on the toilet, in work, on the bus and even on a Christmas day. Someone died when they were electrocuted by a hand dryer in MacDonalds and every day thousands of other people die in the most bizarre circumstances Death is not a laughing matter, especially for those with lots of living to do. We have to make light of the darkest things that can happen to us, it's what makes us human. The only thing you can do is make every day count and every holiday count even more.

CHAPTER 22

Don't Disturb the Neighbours

Lifting the tone somewhat, i will make amends with my favourite holiday story of all time. My late father and his wife were great travellers. They enjoyed life to the full and also went to see all the big stars in concert including regular visits to the theatre. Without doubt they lived with a can do attitude. Even in their later years they were not afraid to travel to places such as Egypt, Mexico and Australia, to name but a few. Their age didn't stop them from visiting exotic locations and they were definitely not the type to sit on a beach all day in Benidorm. They had booked to go to Egypt back in 2011, but due to the uprising and violent demonstrations, the British government advised against travel to the country. Those people with holidays already booked at the popular resorts of Sharm El Sheikh were advised to cancel and book another holiday with their tour operator. Following this advice my mother and father in law did exactly that and swapped their five star luxury hotel for a two week stay in Gran Canaria. Slightly disappointed with their last minute change, they decided to make the most of all that Gran Canaria had to offer, including the like for like five star hotel. Unfortunately, the change of destination meant that there were no daytime flights left on the day of their departure and they were left with no choice but to take a late evening flight. Arriving after midnight to their hotel meant that the check in was a subdued affair without the usual welcoming drinks or the glimpses of the hotel pool in all its glory. When telling us this story they explained to me that a Spanish porter reluctantly picked up their suitcases and led them through the grounds of the hotel and up a flight of outdoor steps. He never spoke a word and quietly opened a door exposing a large room, nicely decorated with a large double bed. There was an en-suite bathroom including shower toilet and bathrobes. The room had a television, tea making facilities and even a small fridge. There was a built in wardrobe and drawers for clothing, but there was no escaping how compact the room was. They initially complained to reception about the cost they'd paid for the holiday and the standard of room they'd been given but were told that being a last minute booking they were lucky to get this room at such short notice.

They eventually became friendly with a few other guests over a drink at the pool bar and during conversation explained their downgraded experience. This brought about sympathy and condemnation from other guests who'd paid far less. On the fourth day my mother in law noticed the cleaner had left the adjoining door to their room slightly open and asked my father in law to take a look inside. Uncomfortable with this request he slowly stepped into the adjoining room being careful not to disturb or move anything. Having been encouraged to grab some cutlery he was left almost speechless when he became more confident to take a closer look at the rest of the room and its features. When he returned back to his own room, he was furious. 'They've got everything next door it's huge and spacious compared to ours, we need to complain again,' he insisted.

This time they called reception using the bedside phone, who in turn sent up a manager that met them already standing angrily by the door. He asked them what it was they didn't like about the apartment and led them around the balcony towards another door. Opening the door, he began waving his arms around gesturing for them to find fault with the magnificent view from the private balcony. The room had a double fridge, a huge television and was beautifully furnished top to bottom. The manager then opened the door to the bedroom and told them 'this is one of our largest bedrooms on the complex.' This was the room my mother and father in law had been living in for the past four days. They were mortified and beyond embarrassed then they explained to the manager that they had assumed the bedroom had been their whole apartment. The more they told me with a straight face the more I laughed, there is something even more satisfying when it's the in-laws. To be fair they also saw the funny side and I can almost justify their mistake. I've stayed on cruise ships with doors between rooms that are designed to host two sets of occupants or one family. The cruel side of me couldn't help but think, what if they'd have done the full two weeks in the bedroom and only discovered their mistake on the last day. Now that would have been a better story!

CHAPTER 23

Life and Lemons

The word holiday is taken from the religious event, holy day. It signifies a day when a person is exempt from work. It has been used by many faiths and religions to celebrate an important date in the calendar. The working class today have now acquired far more leisure time than our grandparents ever had. Go back through history and you will find that most people were lucky to spend a Sunday afternoon in the park after a Sunday morning in a church. Working six days a week was common practice for most families and this lasted well into the seventies. Bank holidays only came into existence in 1871 and it took until the nineteen thirties to introduce a mandatory week's holiday as law. By the fifties two weeks annual leave had become standard and today most workers expect at least four weeks holiday entitlement. This in turn helped create a huge financial market for travelling abroad and as a nation we try desperately to take advantage of our ability to see the world. Little did we realise that the recent pandemic would bring the holiday world crashing to its knees. We are still feeling the after effects of Covid 19 today and there are no strong signs of recovery. Airports lost their staff instead of suitcases and there's nobody wanting the job of loading those suitcases onto a carousel. Brexit certainly made its mark on the workplace throughout the U.K. as our European workforce headed home and left Britain to *laterally* flow it alone. I'm not trying to fly the flag as a pro European, but it was from here that many people filled important roles within the NHS, farms and care homes. We lost many other professionals who topped up the shortfall that the U.K. struggles to fill in certain skilled occupations. It is no coincidence that the holiday companies are in disarray with strike action and cancellations becoming widespread at the time of writing.

Through skilful advertising we are constantly offered a lot more choice when it comes to foreign holidays, yet some holiday companies are struggling to service them. Cruise ships have been parked up for years due to Covid and they already had a constant battle of their own with the common and dreaded Norovirus.

Thankfully May 2022 started to see the relaxation of having to provide added documentation when traveling abroad. The fear of having to isolate in a government designated hotel on your return was enough to frighten most people away from booking a hotel anywhere abroad. As the rules started to relax regarding the quarantine laws and the necessity of taking a PCR test, my wife and i decided to take a trip to Corfu.

We stayed at an all-inclusive hotel a few kilometres from Corfu old town in an area known as Kommeno. The Eva Palace is a truly stunning hotel, the pool, private beach and surrounding views were all outstanding. The staff were amazingly polite and professional and while dining away from the hotel one evening, some staff recognised us and bought us drinks, how often does that happen? We hired a car, and it broke down halfway up a mountain with smoke billowing from the engine. The hire car company gave us half of our money back so we couldn't really complain. Everything was perfect, except it was too perfect. Nothing happened, the other guests were quiet and respectful, and the day was as relaxed as you could get. I read a book and we walked a few miles each day. The only exciting thing apart from being stranded half way up a mountain was the fridge turning into an oven and getting dragged away by a maintenance man. Did I mention the guy who excitedly told us how great he feels after his hip operation and did his own version of the 'can can' by the pool as if to prove a point? it's criminal to think that i couldn't find anything exciting to write about when it's a perfect holiday. The truth is we long for the perfect holiday it's what the commercials desperately try to sell us. The same people who couldn't care less when they cancel the flight at the last minute. The advert that grabbed your attention had sun-tanned people frolicking around an empty pool while holding decorative cocktails and being served conveniently by the smiling hotel manager at the empty beach bar. The brochure or TV advert that advertises the hotel also has the same two people having a well prepared meal in an empty restaurant surrounded by smiling waiters and someone playing a violin. Busy as he is preparing eye catching meals, the chef has found time to pop out and say hello, just for you. He has a moustache that curls up at each end and his chef's hat is starched to attention. Pick up any holiday brochure or surf the net and the photos on the web site will have the same rules applied. The first thing you will notice is it's always a blue sky with no clouds in sight. There is always a distant photograph of the pool and the tidy rows of unoccupied sun loungers. All humans have been evaporated as the marketers don't want you to think of lying next to Chantelle trout pout and mouth almighty Baz and their three kids, Britney, Candice and Kyle. If the commercial includes any family entertainment, it's guaranteed that the closest thing to the Von Trap family are flashing their bright white teeth as they sing along to the reps version of 'Grease.' A giant Pepper Pig is cuddling the child model while six pack dad is leaping to hit the volleyball back to mum, Miss Albania 2020. The room is modern bright and comfortable, and you wouldn't see a speck of dust even if you used the Hubble telescope. However, the other three hundred rooms are cleaned regularly by Dynorod and the Pied Piper of Hamlin. Great company by the way unblocked my drains superbly, they know the meaning of 'doing a solid.'

When Covid first raised its ugly spiked proteins, many people had bought and paid in full for their future holidays. I listened to terrible stories regarding well known companies refusing to refund customers, stating that it could take months to sort out. Some of those well known companies started offering vouchers instead of a refund, thus ensuring you rebooked with them and them only. Suddenly we started to see the unthinkable, Thomas Cook and Flybe went bust. Virgin started asking for financial help and the famous 'Teletext Holidays,' liquidated due to court action in 2021 for not being able to refund customers. The sad part of all this was that these companies were not entirely to blame. People who had the symptoms of Covid cancelled their holidays in droves, along with those who feared a restricted holiday due to mask wearing and social distancing. The whole travel concept was buggered. Back home you had to sit apart on a bus or a train while wearing a mask and only one person was allowed in an elevator in the workplace. Family bubbles became the social norm, and we couldn't meet at funerals, pubs or even in the garden during its strictest point. I could give my daughter a lift to work but even though we worked in the same place we couldn't get in the lift together. The camping industry went through a boom as people realised that the only way to get away as a family was in a tent in a field. The camp site owners had their own problems, having to close off facilities and washrooms. People went mad for turning their gardens into their own getaways with jacuzzis and homemade wooden bars appearing all over social media. Boris Johnson and some of his cabinet members did the opposite and broke the rules on a regular basis and 'party gate' became the scandal in the aftermath of Covid. We have watched the government imploding on itself, and our country looks to be heading towards a recession.

It now seems that we are destined to live with some form of Covid for the foreseeable future and as it mutates and creates new types of infection, we learn to live alongside it's alien presence. For some entrepreneurs Covid brought massive opportunities especially in the PPE market. The government can testify to that, having spent ten billion pounds of taxpayers money on unusable equipment and writing it off. For others there were job losses, and we began to read stories of airline pilots stacking shelves in supermarkets and cabin crews who took to working for delivery companies and taking low paid jobs.

The fact that they did this shows their resolve and courage and speaks volumes to their character and let's be honest, many of them probably had mouths to feed. So, where do we go from here, what is the future of the Great British holiday and our beloved travel to the corners of the earth? Will the day come when we will just have to be happy with a virtual holiday? A headset and an artificial sea breeze blowing across your face. Will the oceans be so full of plastic that we no longer want to go to the beach because the sand lies somewhere beneath a blanket of plastic waste? Will global warming have such an effect on the earth that the polar ice caps will finally melt, and Holland will be transformed into its very own version of Atlantis. The Shetland islands could become the equivalent of the canary islands, while the rest of Scotland celebrates being the holiday hot spot of the world. Meanwhile down in Greece they're having the annual sled race from the Acropolis to the Colosseum straight across the frozen Mediterranean. Bono said there won't be snow in Africa,' but how long before he's wrong? Thousands of children's letters could end up being delivered to the snow covered pyramids and Santa's new home. The future is unmistakably in our own hands.

Today's date is the 12th July 2022, and it has been announced that Heathrow Chief Executive John Holland Kaye has asked airlines to stop selling flights as they cannot handle the one hundred thousand passengers already passing through its terminals on a daily basis. Conveniently and I couldn't have timed this any better, yesterday was the 11th July and it saw China suffering from unusually high and excessive heat causing roads to buckle and people to seek cooler temperatures in some underground air raid shelters. As temperatures of more than forty degrees are expected, eighty six cities including Shanghai have been placed on red alert. Meanwhile back here in the U.K. there is an amber alert for extreme heat expected on Sunday for temperatures to rise above 38.7 Celsius.

After what felt like the most miserable June ever, it's more than welcome. The news will be full of stories showing people packing out the beaches, usually Brighton for some weird reason. They never fail to bring a clip of a couple of old ladies dipping their feet in Trafalgar Square. There'll be the old quotes telling us we're ten degrees hotter than Athens and that some village in Cornwall has broken the record for average temperature since records began. You can guarantee there'll be a disaster element to the news, just to act as a warning. Hospitals have reported high levels of people with of severe cases of sunburn, especially in Scotland. Meanwhile in Wales, mountain rescue teams came to the aid of a dozen people from Manchester who were climbing Snowdon in flip flops, bikinis and carrying a case of Stella Artois. They didn't do this in the 1920's no sir. A day out to Wales from Manchester or Liverpool in one of those old coaches was a fifteen miles per hour fun fest. The Charabanc was effectively a party on wheels, with drunken revellers throwing not only bottles but sometimes themselves onto the road. It was similar to a single deck bus with no roof and as dangerous a mode of transport you will ever find. At 15mph it would take at least five hours to get to the North Wales seaside town of Llandudno from Liverpool and of course the same time to get back, leaving little time to enjoy the resort. The roads were usually in poor condition and should the Charabanc accidentally turn over, there would be terrible and fateful injuries. Nothing could have been worse than sitting in one of these seats for five hours especially in miserable weather conditions. People longed to get away from the dreadful city smog and the acrid smell of the factories, so this was a welcome burden for the poorest of pilgrims.

We have long been considered as a nation of traveller's and explorers who throughout history, opened the eyes of the world to what lies beyond the horizon. Although Sir Francis Drake was the second person to circumnavigate the earth, he well and truly expanded the distances previously covered by some upstart called Ferdinand Magellan. Not only that, but he also created some red hot trade routes, a bit like Amazon and Apple by today's standards. Good old England gave the rest of the world bags of wool, and they gave us spices, slaves and gold. The gold bit we sort of stole off the Spanish along the way. We were first to climb Everest while someone else carried the bags. It's what we do best, it's what we're all about on this island, were full of eccentric people and shopkeepers. The fact that we are a country surrounded by water defines who we are and our passion for adventure. For some its about sitting in a bar in Benidorm or having a Margarita in Mexico, because we are the lovers of a good old knees up and a party. From getting on a banana boat, to boarding the Titanic, it's a contract we make in good faith and accept our fate. There are no guarantees that you won't get held hostage because you happen to be in a quaint village in Bolivia. The simple rule for going on a holiday is to always expect the unexpected. There are still active volcanoes losing their temper every now and again and throwing ash clouds high into the air. The animals you may see in a zoo over here are roaming free over there. Spiders and snakes in the UK are relatively harmless and the latter is nearly impossible to find. In some countries you will find they have ferocious sharks in the water and even more dangerous sharks in the streets. In some places corruption by the authorities is second nature and you can get fined by police patrols for wearing a loud shirt. The old classic food poisoning is never far from making at least one appearance on holiday and before you know it, you're speaking to God on the big white telephone throwing up some modern art and repeatedly saying, 'oh my God.' Therefore I believe the chances of having a carefree holiday are now virtually impossible. Aldous Huxley the philosopher and traveller whom i mentioned earlier at the beginning of this book once said, 'You pays your money you takes your chance.' Isn't there something immensely exciting about that?

Bon voyage!

Printed in Great Britain
by Amazon

30651238R10115